BATHROOM
READS

Publications International, Ltd.

TABLE OF CONTENTS

CHAPTER 1

Lavatory Lore

Restroom, bathroom, washroom . . . we use these nicely vague, utilitarian terms without thinking about them too much. They're descriptive but not too descriptive. They came into common usage not too long ago to meet a social need: to describe a place where people go at certain times to do certain things. While the term *bathroom* can be traced back to the 18th century, the other two words are 19th century coinages.

Plenty of other names arose along the way. If you were dining in a London restaurant at the turn of the last century, you might have been surprised by your companion's sudden departure for the *bog*. Likewise, in New York City, you might have overheard locals noting they would like to "stop at the *necessary*." A century earlier, delicate dandies and ladies of both countries inquired after temples of convenience when they were away from home. The common thread here? Euphemism. Ever since we brought the sanitary comfort facilities indoors, we've used language to distance ourselves from what goes on in there. The English language is filled with some incredibly indirect expressions. "When nature calls" has to rank as one of the most noble-sounding dodges ever. "WC" makes a bland acronym of the already harmless "water closet." And announcing your departure to the throne room or corporate headquarters brings off the event with unlooked-for gravitas.

That said, the man who cleaned the easement privy probably had his own name for it. He would have employed the flip side of the euphemism, the dysphemism. Low elements and heirs to Shakespeare alike have deposited a rich loam of dysphemism over the years. Slop hoppers, crappers (more on that later), shitters, and thunder boxes abound, as do many more truly potty-mouthed contrivances. If only they had all been recorded. Finally, there are those odd, but neutral-sounding terms that have come down to us: latrine, loo, head, can, commode—and the john.

Poor John. Of all the names in the English language, "John" might be applied in the most unflattering ways. What do we call the note that's left by a woman who's jilting her lover? A "Dear John" letter. A prostitute's customer? A john. A colloquial reference to a bathroom? John again. What did John do to deserve so much disrespect?

The most common explanation for why we call the bathroom the john is that it retained an association with the first name of British nobleman Sir John Harington, who invented the flush toilet in the 1590s. While this may be a close enough answer for online trivia sites, it's not really true. Although Harington is, in fact, commonly credited with devising a prototype of the flush toilet, the "john" moniker for the bathroom is almost certainly not related to his achievement.

The evidence for this is legion. First, when Harington invented the toilet, he termed it the "ajax,"—a pun on the term "jakes," which was slang for toilet at the time. Second, the newfangled toilet idea never really caught on during Harington's lifetime—the device didn't come into widespread use until after 1775, when another British inventor, Alexander Cummings, received a patent for it. It seems unlikely that Harrington's name would have been attached to the toilet nearly two centuries after the fact.

Also, consider that "john" as a term for the bathroom isn't recorded in print until the mid-eighteenth century, nearly 150 years after Harington's moment of glory. But what really throws the whole theory into the toilet, however, is that "john" is a distinctly American term—you won't hear people in Britain call the bathroom the "john" any more than you'll hear Americans call it the "WC."

Americans visiting England have learned that this does not mean "welcome center." Nor is it a White Castle or where Winston Churchill lived.

My Cousin Did It

So where does the term come from? Like many slang phrases, its origins aren't entirely clear. The tradition of calling an unknown or metaphorical person "John"—think John Doe, John Barleycorn, or even Johnny-on-the-spot—has been around for centuries.

The first recorded use of the term "john" to refer to the bathroom dates back to 1738 and is found in the rules that governed the actions of incoming Harvard freshmen: "No freshman," the rules say, "shall mingo against the College wall or go into the fellows' cuz john." "Cuz john," etymologists claim, was short for "cousin John," an 18th-century American slang term for the bathroom.

Cousin John's identity is a mystery, although he probably wasn't anybody in particular. Indeed, "going to visit cousin John" was probably a euphemism of the throne room/corporate headquarters variety. The word "mingo," incidentally, was slang for urinating, and it's amusing to note that the college elders found it necessary to enact a rule that prohibited students from peeing on college buildings. On the other hand, it goes to show that the behavior of college students hasn't changed much in almost three centuries.

Sitting Pretty with Mr. Crapper

If there ever was a contest for a person whose career was defined by their name, then Thomas Crapper would win hands down. Crapper was a 19th-century plumber who, despite the urban legend, did not invent the flush toilet. And, although his name has often been associated to the first references of "crap" and "crapper," both terms date back before his career. What Crapper did do was promote and increase the popularity of the flush toilet (a fairly novel invention until some were installed at England's Great Exhibition in 1851), promote sanitary plumbing, and come up with the idea of a bathroom fittings showroom. Crapper's most affluent client was Prince Edward, and he installed all of the plumbing, cedarwood toilet seats, and enclosures (including 30 lavatories) in the prince's country estate.

Though Crapper did not invent the toilet, he did sell a great deal of them in the late 1800s—and each had its tank emblazoned with the Crapper name. In World War I, American soldiers who encountered these toilets while stationed in Europe—some of whom were seeing flush toilets for the first time—simply started using poor Thomas's last name as a nickname for going to the bathroom.

The first public toilets were introduced in 1851 in London's Crystal Palace. Visiting dignitaries were said to be flush with excitement over the innovation. Guests made their way to the Retiring Rooms, and, for a penny, were shown into their very own "Monkey Closets." The term most likely developed from plumbing trade slang, but we encourage wild speculation.

You can't have a toilet without water pipes. Humble hollow tubes have been improving our quality of life for thousands of years. As it turns out, the piping of water in and out of living spaces originated in many different ancient civilizations. Plumbing technology was often developed only to be lost until it was reinvented from scratch. Lead pipes have been found in Mesopotamian ruins, and clay knee joint piping has been traced to Babylonia. The Egyptians used copper piping. But the most sophisticated ancient waterworks flourished at the hands of the Harappan civilization (circa 3300–1600 BC) in the areas of present-day India and Pakistan. The Harappans boasted of a network of earthenware pipes that would carry water from people's homes into municipal drains and cesspools. Archeological excavation uncovered highly planned cities with living quarters featuring individual indoor baths and even toilets.

While the Romans can't be credited with the invention of water pipes, their mastery of pipe-making influenced plumbing up to the 20th century. Pipes were made by shaping sheets of easily malleable (and highly toxic) molten lead around a wooden core. Plumbers then soldered the joints together with hot lead. It could be said that they were largely responsible for "civilizing" Rome, making it a place where homes had bathtubs as well as indoor toilets that flushed into underground sewage systems. Fresh water was piped directly into kitchens, and there were even ways of "metering" how much water was being used by the width of the pipe installed. (Even then, convenience had its price.)

Bathing Is Bad for You, Except When It's Good

Regular bathing is a matter of course these days. Yet as late as 1920, barely one out of a hundred American homes had bathtubs. The lack of bathing facilities wasn't due to inferior technology and pre-modern sanitation. It was mostly a matter of prevailing attitudes. From the time of the Renaissance, most Europeans were wary of bathing—deeming it unhealthy. The terrible plagues of the late Middle Ages may have contributed to hydrophobia. Along with bubonic plague, disseminated by fleas and rats, diseases such as cholera and typhoid were spread by filthy water. The people of the time didn't know about germs but may have intuited the link between bad water and ill health. The phrase "catch your death of cold" arose during an era when there was no hot running water for bathing during cold spells.

By the time of America's colonization, the fear of water had taken firm root. When John Smith and his fellow settlers moved to Jamestown, Virginia, the native Powhatans, who bathed every day, literally held their noses when downwind of the colonists.

Light in Darkness

Contrary to myth, folks in the "Dark Ages" were relatively enlightened about cleanliness. According to the book, *A History of Private Life*, medieval fabliaux—tall tales like those of Chaucer—are replete with lovers taking hot baths before lovemaking. Ladies and lords of the manor soaked on stools placed in wooden vats filled with hot water. They also scrubbed their hands and faces before meals and washed their mouths out after, according to the etiquette guides of the time. The more common folk soaked in urban public baths called "stews," the opening of which were heralded by the sound of trumpet and drum each morning. Doughty burghers marched to the stews naked to stop thieves from picking their pockets. Inside, the two sexes bathed together, sometimes clothed.

The Catholic Church frowned on the mixed-gender aspect, especially when it led to prostitution. Some orders of monks prescribed bathing only for Christmas and Easter, with the private parts covered during these sacred ablutions. But the clergy wasn't totally doctrinaire. The founder of the modern papacy, Pope Gregory I, advised taking a bath each Sunday. And monasteries featured fountains for hand washing.

A noted early scientist, Hildegard of Bingen (1098–1179), offered these prescriptions for good health: "If a person's head has an ailment, it should be washed frequently in this water and it will be healed . . . If your lord wishes to bathe and wash his body clean . . . have a basin full of hot fresh herbs and wash his body with a soft sponge." Along with roses, herbs added to bath water included hollyhock, brown fennel, danewort, chamomile, and green oats. Hildegard also offered this advice for overly randy fellows: "A man who has an overabundance in his loins should cook wild lettuce in water and pour that water over himself in a sauna bath."

Public bathing did continue, but by the 1400s, fires were common in the public baths, where water was heated by the burning of wood. Wood itself was hard to find as growing prosperity led to the leveling of forests. Moreover, peasants often fell ill from the custom of the entire family washing from the same dirty barrel of water. Furthermore, it was believed that disease spread by way of vapors that passed into the skin through pores that opened during bathing. (This is where the term malaria, which means "bad air," comes from.) No less an authority than English philosopher Francis Bacon advised: "After Bathing, wrap the Body in a seare-cloth made of Masticke, Myrrh, Pomander, and Saffron, for staying the perspiration or breathing of the pores." If body odor lingered, courtiers—male and female—cloaked their smell with copious applications of cologne. Yet, attitudes were never monolithic. In the spring of 1511, the diary of one Lucas Rem of Germany reports that he took 127 baths.

Back to early America. Bathing was becoming more accessible and acceptable by the mid-19th century. Millions of the "unwashed masses" were forsaking farms for crowded, filthy cities, and millions more were arriving on immigrant ships. In response, the healthier, better-educated natives crusaded for better health. Healthy living—physical and spiritual—became all the rage. One fad among the wealthy was "taking the waters" at spas such as Saratoga Springs, New York, and Warm Springs, Georgia, the latter of which was frequented by Franklin Roosevelt.

By the mid-1850s, wealthy homes were being designed with their own bathrooms. Victorian excess was not far behind. Decorative embossing and florid coloring led to toilets and basins covered with flower patterns, fruit, and birds, as well as questionable maritime themes (think lumpy dolphins). Bold and showy brass fixtures were also popular.

Executive Privilege

Running water was first installed on the ground floor of the White House in 1833. Upstairs plumbing was introduced 20 years later, during Franklin Pierce's presidency.

Bathrooms began to take their modern appearance after the development of large-scale manufacture of indoor plumbing, toilets, bathtubs, and bathing accoutrements. In the 1880s, the Standard Sanitary Manufacturing Company made cast-iron bathtubs available to the public. These were actually advertised as horse troughs/bathtubs; apparently there were still doubts about how many people would buy a tub only for bathing.

During the boom times of the Roaring Twenties, the urban middle classes, envious of mansions trendily outfitted with indoor plumbing, began putting sinks, toilets, and tubs into separate rooms called bathrooms. It took another decade for electricity and indoor plumbing to reach rural homes.

The Bathroom's Most Essential Accoutrement

Like pasta, gunpowder, and civil service examinations, toilet paper was first invented in China. Paper—made from pulped bamboo and cotton rags—was also invented by the Chinese, although Egyptians had already been using papyrus plants for thousands of years to make writing surfaces. Still, it wasn't until 1391, almost 1,600 years after the invention of paper, that the Ming Dynasty Emperor first used toilet paper. The government made 2 x 3 foot sheets, which either says something about the manufacturing limitations of the day or the Emperor's diet.

Toilet paper didn't reach the United States until 1857 when the Gayetty Firm introduced "Medicated Paper." The product was sold in packages of flat sheets. The sheets were medicated with aloe and featured Gayetty's watermark. Albany inventor Seth Wheeler claimed the patent for toilet paper on a roll in 1871. Although his Albany Perforated Wrapping Paper Company brought their products to the market much earlier, it was the Scott Paper Company that truly brought toilet paper to the masses in 1890. The company employed new manufacturing techniques to introduce perforated sheets. By 1925 they were the leading toilet paper company in the world.

In 1942, Britain's St. Andrew's Paper Mill invented two ply sheets (the civilized world owes a great debt to the Royal Air Force for protecting this London factory during The Blitz). Two ply sheets are not just two single-ply sheets stuck together; each ply in a two ply sheet is thinner than a single ply sheet. The first "moist" toilet paper—Cottonelle Fresh Rollwipes—appeared in 2001.

8.6 Sheets
That's the average number of sheets a consumer uses on a trip to the bathroom. Each American uses about 21,000 sheets each year.

Using What's at Hand

So what did people wipe with before Gayetty, Wheeler, and Scott? It varied. In forested regions it was natural to reach up for a nice, clean, bunch of leaves. Pooping in rivers and then tidying up with water was popular with European commoners, whereas wealthy elites might use pages from a book, hemp, and even lace. If you were near the beach, there were seashells, seaweed, and . . . sand. Snow was sometimes used in cold climates. Moss, bark, sticks, wool and fur, rocks . . . there are records of just about every common material being used.

In the days of the Roman Empire, commoners would attach sponges to sticks and soak them in saltwater. When they were done, the sponges would be placed back in the saltwater for the next person. There is little information about what happened when the stick poked through the sponge, but the Romans were a hearty, expansionist people and probably conquered another country for spite.

During the Middle Ages, European farmers were fond of using balls of hay. American pioneers did the same. They also saved their corncobs in baskets for a little wiping variety. Later, they began saving the pages of their Farmer's Almanacs and Sears and Roebucks catalogs.

Let's Get Rolling

Toilet paper comes from trees. Preferred trees include Southern pines and Douglas firs (for long fibers that give paper strength) and maple and oak trees (for shorter fibers that make paper softer). Typically, toilet paper is a combination of 70% hardwood and 30% softwood.

The wood is barked, chipped, mixed with a slurry, and poured into a giant pressure cooker. Out of this comes a pulp which gets further refined, eventually resulting in a paper stock which is sprayed on screens and dried. After drying, the paper is creped, a process that softens and wrinkles it.

Quality is usually determined by the number of plies. One ply has a single sheet and it's usually the cheapest option. Two ply consists of two layers that have been bonded together. Premium toilet paper is usually made of superior pulped paper, has two to four plies, and may also be treated with lotion.

The Bidet

That thing in there—what is it? How do you use it? Is it a toilet that began changing itself into a drinking fountain before deciding to become a birdbath?

The word *bidet* is apt. It's French for "pony." When you use the bidet, you're straddling it like a little horse. Bluntly put, it's a plumbing fixture that lets you use water to wash your butt after you've used the toilet. Bidets have been around for centuries in some other countries, but they're not widely used in the United States—which is kind of odd when you consider Americans' concern with cleanliness. You'll commonly find them in Europe (97% of Italian households have them), and they're very popular in South America, the Middle East, and parts of Asia as well.

The Italians and French developed and began refining the bidet in the 18th century. At first they were used as complements to chamber pots, and kept in bedrooms. The *bidet à seringue* appeared around 1750. It gave users a nice upward spray, which they controlled with a hand pump. Centuries later, when indoor plumbing started to catch on, the bidet moved into the bathroom. Knobs and sprayers replaced the old hand pump. Today, electric bidets feature undreamed-of luxury: water temperature controls, heated seats, warm air dryers, and even deodorant appliers can be purchased.

So again—why don't Americans use these lovely, hygienic appliances? Some historians suspect the bidet's connection with France is to blame. During the two world wars of the 20th century, American soldiers in France would have seen bidets in brothels. They may have returned home associating bidets with immorality. There also may be some lingering Francophobia—passed on to us from the English—that makes us reject anything that seems overly effete and pronounced with a nasal accent.

Wildlife in the Plumbing

Have you ever felt an irrational fear that some slime-coated creature might come swimming, crawling, or flying out of the toilet? Well, guess what? You're not so irrational after all! Yes indeed, snakes and rats do sometimes get into the pipes and slither and squirm around in there like kittens under a silk sheet. Sorry if you're sitting down right now, but there's more—some of those critters have even reached up and bitten people who were just trying to do their business.

Unwanted Visitors

There are two ways for an animal to make its way up into your toilet. First, if your house is connected to a municipal sewer system, the drain leading from your toilet connects to a large network of pipes that go all the way to a sewer treatment plant. This network has many small entry points, including manholes and other people's toilets.

Because of the food everyone washes down the sink, these pipes are popular hangouts for rats; because there are delicious rats everywhere, the pipes also are popular with snakes. Water rarely fills the pipes all the way and usually moves slowly, so snakes and rats can come and go as they please. Every once in a while, a snake or a rat will follow a pipe all the way to a toilet, swim through the little bit of water in the bowl, and pop out to see what's going on.

The second way in is much quicker. Most houses have vents that run from the sewage drainpipes to the roof. These allow noxious sewer gas to escape without stinking up the inside of the house. If these vents aren't covered, rats, snakes, frogs, and even squirrels can fall in and land unexpectedly in the main drain line. They scurry for the nearest exit: the toilet. (It's probably a good idea to cover those vents if you haven't already.)

Tales from the Bowl

There have been many reported cases of unexpected toilet visitors, including a venomous water moccasin that bit a Jacksonville, Florida woman in 2005 and a baby brush-tailed possum that crawled out of a toilet in Brisbane, Australia, in 2008. If you have a snake phobia, the creepiest story might be that of Keith, a ten-foot-long boa constrictor that kept poking out of toilets in an apartment building in Manchester, England, in 2005. The snake, a pet that its owner had set free after being evicted, lived the high life, eating sewer rats and freaking people out for months before a building resident lured him into a bucket.

Eight Famous People Who Died in the Bathroom

When these people said they had to go, they weren't kidding. All of these people ended their time on Earth in the bathroom—some accidentally, others intentionally. One thing is for certain—none of them got a chance to wash their hands before leaving.

Elvis Presley

On January 8, 1935, Elvis Presley, King of Rock 'n' Roll, was born in Tupelo, Mississippi. He was discovered in Memphis by Sun Records founder Sam Phillips, who was looking for a white singer with an African-American sound and style.

Elvis catapulted to fame following three appearances on *The Ed Sullivan Show* in 1956 and 1957. Although he was pushed off the charts by The Beatles and the rest of the British invasion in the early 1960s, he still sold more than a billion records in his lifetime, more than any other recording artist in history. His movie career kept him in the public eye until his comeback album in 1968. In the 1970s, he sold out shows in Las Vegas as an overweight caricature of his former self. Elvis's addiction to prescription drugs was well known, and on August 16, 1977, he was found dead on the bathroom floor in his Graceland mansion. A vomit stain on the carpet showed that he had become sick while seated on the toilet and had stumbled to the spot where he died. A medical examiner listed the cause of death as cardiac arrhythmia caused by ingesting a large number of drugs.

Lenny Bruce

Controversial comedian Lenny Bruce was born Leonard Alfred Schneider in October 1925. Bruce was famous in the 1950s and 1960s for his satirical routines about social themes of the day, including politics, religion, race, abortion, and drugs. His use of profanity—rarely done at that time—got him arrested numerous times. He was eventually convicted on obscenity charges, but was freed on bail. On August 3, 1966, Bruce, a known drug addict, was found dead in the bathroom of his Hollywood Hills home with a syringe, a burned bottle cap, and other drug paraphernalia. The official cause of death was acute morphine poisoning caused by an accidental overdose.

Elagabalus

Scandalous 3rd-century Roman emperor Elagabalus married and divorced five women, including a Vestal Virgin (a holy priestess), who under Roman law should have been buried alive for losing her virginity. Elagabalus also may have been bisexual. Objecting to his sexual behavior and his habit of forcing others to follow his religious customs, his grandmother Julia Maesa and aunt Julia Avita Mamaea murdered Elagabalus and his mother (Julia Maesa's own daughter) in the emperor's private latrine. Their bodies were dragged through the streets of Rome and thrown into the Tiber River.

Robert Pastorelli

Born in 1954, actor and former boxer Robert Pastorelli was best known as Candace Bergen's housepainter on the late 80s sitcom *Murphy Brown*. He had numerous minor roles on television and also appeared in *Dances with Wolves*, *Sister Act 2*, and *Michael*, as well as a number of made-for-TV movies. Pastorelli struggled with drug use and in 2004 was found dead on the floor of his bathroom of a suspected heroin overdose.

Orville Redenbacher

Orville Redenbacher, founder of the popcorn company that bears his name, was born in 1907, in Brazil, Indiana. Millions came to know him through his folksy television commercials for the specialty popcorn he invented. He sold the company to Hunt-Wesson Foods in 1976, but remained as a spokesperson until September 20, 1995, when he was found dead in a whirlpool bathtub in his condominium, having drowned after suffering a heart attack.

Claude François

Claude François was a French pop singer in the 1960s who had a hit with an adaptation of Trini Lopez's folk song "If I Had a Hammer." On March 11, 1978, François' obsession with cleanliness did him in when he was electrocuted in the bathroom of his Paris apartment as he tried to fix a broken light bulb while standing in a water-filled bathtub.

Albert Dekker

Actor Albert Dekker, who appeared in *Kiss Me Deadly*, *The Killers*, and *Suddenly, Last Summer*, was on the infamous Hollywood blacklist for several years after criticizing anticommunist Senator Joe McCarthy. Dekker later made a comeback, but in May 1968, he was found strangled to death in the bathroom of his Hollywood home. He was naked, bound hand and foot, with a hypodermic needle sticking out of each arm and obscenities written all over his body. The official cause of death was eventually ruled to be accidental asphyxiation.

Jim Morrison

Born on December 8, 1943, Jim Morrison was best known as the lead singer for The Doors, a top rock band in the late 1960s. His sultry looks, suggestive lyrics, and onstage antics brought him fame, but drug and alcohol abuse ended his brief life. On July 3, 1971, Morrison was found dead in his bathtub in Paris. He reportedly had dried blood around his mouth and nose and bruising on his chest, suggesting a massive hemorrhage brought on by tuberculosis. The official report listed the cause of death as heart failure, but no autopsy was performed because there was no sign of foul play.

Taking Care of Business in Outer Space

Weightlessness sure seems fun. You see those astronauts effortlessly floating around, mugging for the camera, and magically spinning their pens in midair. But what you don't get to see is what happens when nature calls.

The Final Frontier

You can be sure that as much as astronauts enjoy swimming through the air like waterless fish, there's one place on Earth where all astronauts thank their lucky stars for gravity: the bathroom.

On space shuttles, the astronaut sat on a commode with a hole in it, not unlike a normal toilet—except for the restraints that fit over the feet and thighs to prevent his or her body from floating away. Suction took the place of gravity, so the seat was cushioned, which allowed the astronaut's posterior to form an airtight seal around the hole. If everything was situated properly, the solid waste went down the main hole: A separate tube with a funnel on the end took care of the liquids. With so much going on, relaxing with a newspaper is not really an option.

Today's astronauts have it easy compared to their forebears on the Apollo missions (1961–1975). When an Apollo astronaut had to go number two, he attached a specially designed plastic bag to his rear end. The bag had an adhesive flange at its opening to ensure a proper seal.

But if you think that this procedure couldn't have been any more undignified, consider this: There was no privacy. The astronauts would usually carry on with their business while they were, you know, doing their business. In the words of Apollo astronaut Rusty Schweickart, "You just float around for a while doing things with a bag on your butt." With no gravity and no suction, getting the feces to separate from the body was, generally, an hour-long process. It began with removing the bag—very carefully—and ended with lots and lots of wiping.

Waste Management

Where does all this stuff go? Fecal material is dried, compressed, and stored until the ship returns to Earth. (Some scientists believe that manned missions to Mars will require waste to be recycled and used for food. If you were hoping to sign up for one of those flights, you may want to think about that before dropping off your application.) Urine, on the other hand, is expelled into space. The memory of this procedure caused Schweickart to wax darn-near poetic, calling a urine dump at sunset, "one of the most beautiful sights" he saw in space.

"As the stuff comes out and hits the exit nozzle," Schweickart went on, "it instantly flashes into ten million little ice crystals, which go out almost in a hemisphere. The stuff goes in every direction, all radially out from the spacecraft at relatively high velocity. It's surprising, and it's an incredible stream of . . . just a spray of sparklers almost. It's really a spectacular sight."

Why Do People Sing in the Shower?

At recording studios, engineers spend thousands of dollars on foam, ceiling tiles, and other sound-deadening equipment in an attempt to remove as much echo from the room as possible. Sometimes it's all for naught. When the latest scantily clad pop sensation shows up to record an album, the engineers might find themselves electronically goosing the tracks with echo effects, augmenting a voice that is a little less robust than the adoring public might guess.

They could've saved all that money and just recorded the song in the bathroom. With its close quarters and hard, smooth surfaces, the bathroom acts as an echo chamber—sounds are sustained a little longer than normal as they bounce freely around the room. People who are already in love with the sounds of their own voices (you know who you are) find that the echoes make their singing seem fuller and more resonant.

This brand of vanity-enhanced vanity is apparently an international phenomenon. In 2007 a television network in India began producing an amateur talent show called *Bathroom Singer*, in which contestants sang in a bathroom stage setting for cash prizes. Those who didn't show enough *jhaag* (it sounds dirty, but it really just refers to being entertaining) were rudely eliminated from the competition with the sound of a toilet flush.

CHAPTER 2

When Animals Walk into Bars

No, we're not talking about you in your college days. We're talking about the sneaky, irreverent critters that don't respect our boundaries. They're ingenious at inserting themselves into our homes and offices, sneaking rides on our planes, and even braving hostile metropolitan environments. In 2007, a young coyote somehow made its way through the densely populated sidewalks of downtown Chicago to a Quizno's Subs sandwich shop. Finding the door open, it casually sauntered in, climbed into a beverage cooler, and made itself at home. Was it waiting for someone to bring a bottle opener?

In 2012, a young mountain lion tried to sneak into a casino in Reno, Nevada, but couldn't navigate the tricky revolving door. The lion skulked around for a while before parking itself by some stairs, where it loitered until the authorities came to remove it. A wildlife specialist on the scene described the young cat's behavior as "almost the equivalent of being a stupid teenager."

Beginning in 2007, a gang of turkeys in Davis, California took to vandalizing property and intimidating residents. After years of being the main course, it seems they decided to mount a counterattack. At first the ne'er-do-well fowl preferred hanging out in a local cemetery, only venturing out to hassle cyclists and joggers. Soon, however, the three-foot-birds were taking on slow-moving trucks and obstructing the delivery of household mail. One turkey, known as Downtown Tom (we're not making this up), liked to hang out in a bank parking lot, waiting for people to get out of their cars. He would then chase, circle, and lunge at bank patrons. One victim who was chased into a corner called 911: "Hi, um, (gobble) I got a turkey here that just won't let me leave . . . It just put me in a corner and I can't exactly go anywhere." In the audio's background, a hostile turkey can be heard giving its own version of events. As of 2016, most of the turkeys were still at large.

Animals are just as ingenious at extracting themselves from the environments we try to keep them in—boxes, cages, sanctuaries—and zoos. In 2009, more than 5,000 visitors were evacuated from Great Britain's Chester Zoo in the city of Liverpool. "Chimps Gone Wild!" the headlines screamed the next morning. Apparently, 30 chimpanzees had escaped from their island enclosure. The great breakout wasn't necessarily cause for alarm, however. The chimps got no further than the area where their food was kept. They gorged themselves until they had to lie down and rub their aching bellies. A little later, zoo wardens rounded them up, and the escapees returned to their island peacefully.

When it comes to zoo escapes, primates are often among the prime offenders. One of the greatest of all primate escape artists was the legendary Fu Manchu of Omaha's Henry Doorly Zoo. Back in 1968, this orangutan confounded his keepers by repeatedly escaping from his cage no matter how well it was secured. Only when a worker noticed Fu slipping a shiny wire from his mouth did the hairy Houdini's secret come out. The orangutan had fashioned a "key" from this wire and was using it to pick the lock. What's even more impressive is that he had the sense to hide it between his teeth and jaw—a place no one was likely to look. Once officials realized what the cagey animal had been up to, they stripped his cage of wires. Though Fu Manchu never escaped again, he was rewarded for his efforts with an honorary membership in the American Locksmiths Association.

Oliver, a capuchin monkey in Mississippi's Tupelo Buffalo Park and Zoo, went Fu Manchu one better. In 2007, he escaped from his cage twice in three weeks. Both times he traveled several miles before being apprehended. Zookeepers suspected him of picking the lock, but they never figured out how he did it. Their solution was to secure his cage with three locks, a triple threat that has so far kept him inside. Word of Oliver's escapades drew so many visitors to the zoo that officials decided to capitalize on the capuchin culprit. A best-selling item at the zoo's gift shop is a T-shirt emblazoned with "Oliver's Great Escape" along with a map of his routes.

Evelyn, a gorilla at the Los Angeles Zoo, didn't need to pick a lock. She escaped on October 11, 2000, via climbing vines, à la Tarzan. After clambering over the wall of her enclosure, she strolled around the zoo for about an hour. Patrons were cleared from the area, and Evelyn's brief attempt to experience the zoo from a visitor's point of view ended when she was tranquilized and returned to her enclosure without further incident.

Juan, a 294-pound Andean spectacled bear at Germany's Berlin Zoo, had a much more amazing adventure on August 30, 2004. It started when he paddled a log across the moat that surrounded his enclosure. He then scaled the wall and wandered off to the zoo's playground. There, he acted just like a kid, taking a quick spin on the merry-go-round and trying out the slide. When he left in search of further amusement, clever animal handlers decided to distract him with a bicycle. Sure enough, Juan stopped to examine the two-wheeler as if he were contemplating a ride. Before he could make his escape, however, an officer shot him with a tranquilizer dart, thus ending Juan's excellent adventure.

And finally, in Stuttgart, Germany, a seemingly well-organized group of lobsters used their wits and claws to break out of their supermarket crates under the cover of darkness. They then hustled through the front door and down the sidewalk, presumably heading for the ocean. Someone tipped off the police however, and shortly after 1:45 a.m., the crustaceans were apprehended.

Capuchin. Recidivist. These words mean the same thing to the authorities.

On Monday, November 9, 1874, New Yorkers awoke to shocking news. According to the *New York Herald*, enraged animals had broken out of the Central Park Zoo the preceding Sunday. At that very moment, a leopard, cheetah, panther, and other beasts of prey roamed the park in search of hapless victims. Women and children huddled indoors. Men rushed out with rifles, prepared to defend their families. But it was all for naught—the whole story was a hoax perpetuated by a reporter irate at what he thought were lax security measures at the zoo. He was on to something.

Breaking and Entering and Snacking

You've probably heard that an octopus is capable of unscrewing the lid of a jar with its tentacles. You've probably also wondered if it's just an urban legend. Well, rest assured—it's true. The evidence can be found on YouTube. As Strauss's *Thus Spake Zarathustra* swells in the background, Violet the octopus unfurls a snaky tentacle and grasps a closed jar that contains a crab. Then, much like a skilled magician draping a handkerchief over a top hat, it covers the jar with its body. A few minutes later, the jar reemerges . . . without the lid. Or the crab.

Violet isn't the only octopus that can perform this nifty trick. Octi, a resident of New Zealand's National Aquarium, regularly entertains visitors with its ability to extract food from a variety of sealed jars. According to the aquarium's staff, Octi is a friendly, gentle creature that enjoys playing with toys and often reaches out to touch the hands of its keepers—at least when there are no jars around to work on.

How It's Done

An octopus relies on suction to unscrew a lid. The underside of an octopus's arms and body are covered with highly sensitive suction cups that each contain up to 10,000 neurons. These cups convey a wealth of information to the brain, allowing the octopus to vary pressure on the lid and eventually twist it off.

In the wild, an octopus can pry open the most stubborn clam. But since potential meals don't come packed in jars at the bottom of the ocean, the question naturally arises: How does an octopus learn that these strange glass cylinders in the zoo are a source of snacks? The answer: It uses its natural curiosity and plenty of smarts.

Though they may not look very bright, octopuses, also known as cephalopods, are among the intellectual giants of the deep. They have the largest brains of all invertebrates relative to body weight. Their brains are divided into lobes and resemble those of birds or mammals more closely than they do those of fish. Jennifer Mather, a psychologist at Canada's University of Lethbridge, has conducted studies that suggest that octopuses can even be right-eyed or left-eyed, much like humans, who are neurologically wired to favor the right or left hand.

Other Tricks

Mather is a pioneer in the field of octopus intelligence. She believes that octopuses have distinct personalities and are adept at some relatively complex tasks. What's more, biologist Jean Boal of Millersville University in Pennsylvania has tested their navigational skills with underwater mazes and has given them high marks for geographical memory.

And when it comes to camouflage, they're champs, according to cephalopod expert Roger Hanlon. At the Woods Hole Marine Biological Laboratory in Massachusetts, he has observed an octopus quickly change shape and color, transforming itself into an innocent-looking rock drifting along the ocean floor. What's the I.Q. of an average octopus? This is a mystery scientists are still trying to solve.

Rogue Carnival Trucks Always Take the Blame

Residents of the town of Peninsula, Ohio reported seeing a giant snake in several different places over a series of months in 1944. But was the "Peninsula Python" a real-life monster or just a hoax?

Giant snakes are no fantasy. Pythons ten feet or more in length are commonly found in South America. Closer to home, South Florida is seeing more than its share of sensationally large serpents as owners cast unwanted pets into the wild. Unlike Florida, Ohio isn't famous for its weird flora and fauna. However, one of the state's most enduring legends is the so-called "Peninsula Python," a snake of frightening proportions that terrorized the town of Peninsula in the mid-1940s, and whose offspring, some believe, still inhabit the region's forests and marshes.

No Ordinary Snake

The Peninsula Python first made headlines in June 1944, when a farmer named Clarence Mitchell reported seeing it slithering across his cornfield. According to Mitchell, what he witnessed was no ordinary corn snake—it was at least 18 feet long, and so big around that its trail was the width of a tire track. Two days later, the snake appeared again, this time leaving its huge track across Paul and John Szalay's fields. Two days after that, Mrs. Roy Vaughn called the fire department to report that some sort of giant reptile had climbed a fence, entered her henhouse, and devoured one of her chickens. By then, the residents of Ohio had accepted the snake as real, and both the Cleveland and Columbus zoos offered a reward for its live capture. To calm fears, the Peninsula mayor's office formed a posse to hunt down the snake and bring it in—dead or alive.

Because giant pythons aren't exactly indigenous to Ohio, people speculated as to where the snake may have come from. The most popular theory was that it had escaped from a crashed carnival truck—apparently a common explanation for unusual animal sightings. The town of Peninsula quickly became "snake happy" as sightings of the Peninsula Python continued. On June 25, sirens alerted the posse to a sighting near Kelly Hill, but after searching through the prickly brush for a while, they were told it was a false alarm. Then, on June 27, Mrs. Pauline Hopko told authorities that the giant snake had leaped from a willow tree, frightening her, her dogs, and her milk cows, which broke their harnesses and hightailed it for fields afar. On the same day, a group of boys playing also reported seeing the snake.

Sightings became almost commonplace over the next few days. Mrs. Ralph Griffin said the snake reared up in the middle of her backyard, and Mrs. Katherine Boroutick alleged the behemoth fell from her butternut tree while she was getting rid of some trash down by the river. But every time the mayor's posse arrived at the scene of a reported sighting, the snake was nowhere to be found.

Myth or Real Creature?

The Peninsula Python continued to terrorize the residents of Peninsula through the summer and into the fall, when reports suddenly ceased. It was assumed that the bitter Ohio winter ultimately did the snake in, but no evidence of its remains was ever discovered. Was the Python real? Many residents believe so, but others suspect that the whole thing was just a hoax perpetrated by writer Robert Bordner, a local resident whose account of the snake's mysterious appearance was published in the November 1945 issue of *Atlantic Monthly*.

Regardless, the town of Peninsula has heartily embraced the snake, and now celebrates the legend with an annual Peninsula Python Day. The celebration includes food, fun, and festivities such as a Python Scavenger Hunt, face painting, and a display of live snakes from the Akron Zoo—all of which are of normal size.

Bad Animal Jokes

Steve Allen once said something about jokes being a social lubricant for getting over bad spots. These are not that. These jokes will annoy everybody. They're perfect to use on family members, strangers in airports, surly cashiers, and especially teenagers.

A dog with only three legs walks into an old western saloon and says, "I'm looking for the man who shot my paw."

A chicken and an egg walk into a pub. The bartender looks up and says, "Is this some kind of joke?"

A dung beetle walks into a bar alone. The bartender says, "Here's a stool for you."

A grasshopper walks into a bar and orders a beer. The bartender brings it over and says, "Hey did you know there's a drink named after you?" "Really?" the grasshopper replies. "There's a drink called Randy?"

A termite walks into a bar and says, "Where's the bar tender?"

A little pig walks into a bar, asks for a beer and asks where the bathroom is. The bartender points it out to him and the pig hurries off. A second little pig then comes in, orders a drink and asks for the bathroom. The bartender points it out again and the pig hurries away. A third little pig then appears and orders a drink. "I suppose you want to know where the toilets are," the bartender says. "Not really," replies the pig. "I just go wee-wee-wee all the way home."

A cat walks into a bar. Then walks out of the bar. Then back in. Then out again.

A chicken walks into a bar. The bartender says, "We don't serve poultry in here." The chicken replies, "That's okay, I just want a beer."

Nature's Nerds

It's notoriously difficult to gauge intelligence, both in humans and animals. Comparing animal IQs is especially tricky, since different species may be wired in completely different ways. But when you look broadly at problem-solving and learning ability, several animal brainiacs do stand out from the crowd.

Great Apes. Scientists generally agree that after humans, the smartest animals are our closest relatives: chimpanzees, gorillas, orangutans, and bonobos (close cousins to the common chimpanzee). All of the great apes can solve puzzles, communicate using sign language and keyboards, and use tools. Chimpanzees even make their own sharpened spears for hunting bush babies, and orangutans can craft hats and roofs out of leaves. One bonobo named Kanzi has developed the language skills of a three-year-old child—and with very little training. Using a computer system, Kanzi can "speak" around 250 words and can understand 3,000 more.

Dolphins and Whales. Dolphins are right up there with apes on the intelligence scale. They come up with clever solutions to complex problems, follow detailed instructions, and learn new information quickly—even by watching television. They also seem to talk to each other, though we don't understand their language. Scientists believe some species use individual "names"—a unique whistle to represent an individual—and that they even refer to other dolphins in "conversation" with each other. Researchers have also observed dolphins using tools. Bottlenose dolphins off the coast of Australia will slip their snouts into sponges to protect themselves from stinging animals and abrasion while foraging for food on the ocean floor. Marine biologists believe whales exhibit similar intelligence levels as well as rich emotional lives.

Elephants. In addition to their famous long memories, elephants appear to establish deep relationships, form detailed mental maps of where their herd members are, and communicate extensively over long distances through low-frequency noises. They also make simple tools, fashioning fans from branches to shoo away flies. Researchers have observed that elephants in a Kenyan national park can even distinguish between local tribes based on smell and clothing. The elephants may be fine with one tribe but wary of the other, and for good reason: That tribe sometimes spears elephants.

Parrots. People see intelligence in parrots more readily than in other smart animals because they have the ability to speak human words. But in addition to their famed verbal abilities, the birds really do seem to have significant brain power. The most famous brainy bird, an African grey parrot named Alex, who died in 2007, exhibited many of the intellectual capabilities of a five-year-old. He had only a 150-word vocabulary, but he knew basic addition, subtraction, spelling, and colors, and had mastered such concepts as "same," "different," and "none."

A customer walks into a pet store and sees an African grey parrot. He walks up to it and says, "Hey! Can you speak, stupid?" The parrot replies, "Yes, can you fly, dummy?"

Monkeys. They're not as smart as apes, but monkeys are no intellectual slouches. For example, macaque monkeys can understand basic math and will come up with specific cooing noises to refer to individual objects. Scientists have also trained them to learn new skills by imitating human actions, including using tools to accomplish specific tasks. They have a knack for politics, too, expertly establishing and navigating complex monkey societies.

Dogs. If you're looking for animal brilliance, you might find it right next to you on the couch. Dogs are good at learning tricks, and they also demonstrate incredible problem-solving abilities, an understanding of basic arithmetic, and mastery of navigating complex social relationships. A 2009 study found that the average dog can learn 165 words, which is on par with a two-year-old child. And dogs in the top 20 percent of intelligence can learn 250 words. Border collies are generally considered the smartest breed, followed by poodles and German shepherds. One border collie, named Rico, actually knows the names of 200 different toys and objects. When his owners ask for a toy by name, he'll go to the next room and retrieve it for them.

. . . And a Few You Didn't Want to Know About

The animal kingdom is vast and varied, full of exotic specimens such as giraffes, penguins, and monkeys. Yet, there are quite a few other inhabitants of the animal kingdom that you've probably never heard of. Here are a few that might fascinate and amaze you . . . or just give you the creeps.

Raccoon Dog: Named for the similarity in appearance to that of a raccoon, this solitary creature is actually an omnivorous member of the canine family. Found in China, Korea, and Japan, the raccoon dog has the least-sharp teeth of the canine family. It also plays dead to avoid predators and other natural enemies.

Cookiecutter Shark: This small shark, infrequently seen by human eyes, has big lips and a belly that glows a pale blue-green color to help camouflage it from prey. Its name comes from the small, cookie-shape bite marks it leaves.

Blobfish: Found lurking in the depths off the coasts of Australia and Tasmania, this strange-looking creature has been called the "most disgusting fish in the world." The blobfish does not have (nor need) muscles because its jellylike flesh is lighter than water, allowing it to simply float in the high-pressure areas of the ocean.

Pistol Shrimp: These striped crustaceans differ from other shrimp in that they have claws of differing sizes, one larger than the other. The pistol shrimp pulls back the larger claw and snaps it shut, producing a loud sound that stuns its prey. It has been said that the noise produced by a colony of these shrimp snapping their claws in unison is so loud it can block the sonar tracking of nearby submarines.

Shoebill: Discovered in the 19th century, this large bird is named for its beak, which is indeed shaped like a shoe. A long-legged, broad-winged relative of the stork, the shoebill stands four feet tall and has a seven-foot-wide wingspan. It also has a sharp hook on the end of its hefty beak, which is used for catching prey such as catfish.

Suckerfooted Bat: A rare, diminutive bat, the suckerfoot is found in the western forests of Madagascar. It has small suction cups on its hands allowing it to attach itself to smooth surfaces as it glides through the forests in search of its next meal.

Yeti Crab: The pincers of this recently discovered crustacean from the depths of the South Pacific Ocean are covered in yellowish, bacteria-filled hair. Scientists hypothesize that the crabs possibly eat the bacteria, or perhaps use it to detoxify poisonous minerals.

Chinese Giant Salamander: This particular salamander, found in the lakes and streams of China, is the world's largest living amphibian. Though its wrinkled appearance is similar to that of other salamanders, this variety can grow to over five feet in length, making it the undisputed king of salamanders.

Shrike: At first glance, this little bird seems gentle and charming; however, the shrike is infamous for catching and impaling its prey (usually insects, lizards, or small mammals) on thorns. This ultimately helps the bird tear its victims apart, for smaller, more manageable meals. The torn carcasses are then left on the thorns, so the shrike can return for later snacks.

Star-Nosed Mole: This lowland-living critter resembles a common mole, but with a nose that resembles a pink, many-armed starfish. Still, those weird nasal tentacles have nearly 100,000 minute touch receptors. Scientists have recently found that the star-nosed mole is also able to sniff underwater, by quickly inhaling the air bubbles that are blown out through its nostrils.

Do Elephants Have Graveyards?

Just as searching for the Holy Grail was a popular pastime for crusading medieval knights, 19th-century adventurers felt the call to seek out a mythical elephant graveyard.

According to legend, when elephants sense their impending deaths, they leave their herds and travel to a barren, bone-filled wasteland. Although explorers have spent centuries searching for proof of these elephant ossuaries, not one has ever been found, and the elephant graveyard has been relegated to the realm of metaphor and legend.

Elephants Never Forget

Unlike most mammals, elephants have a special relationship with their dead. Researchers from the United Kingdom and Kenya have revealed that elephants show marked emotion—from actual crying to profound agitation—when they encounter the remains of other elephants, particularly the skulls and tusks. They treat the bones with unusual tenderness and will cradle and carry them for long periods of time and over great distances. When they come across the bones of other animals, they show no interest whatsoever. Not only can elephants distinguish the bones of other elephants from those of rhinoceroses or buffalo, but they appear to recognize the bones of elephants they were once familiar with. An elephant graveyard, though a good way to ensure that surviving elephants wouldn't be upset by walking among their dead on a daily basis, does not fit with the elephants' seeming sentiment toward their ancestors.

Honor Your Elders

The biggest argument against an elephant burial ground can be found in elephants' treatment of their elders. An elephant would not want to separate itself from the comfort and protection of its herd during illness or infirmity, nor would a herd allow such behavior. Elephants accord great respect to older members of a herd, turning to them as guiding leaders. They usually refuse to leave sick or dying older elephants alone, even if it means risking their own health and safety.

But What About the Bones?

Although there is no foundation for the idea that the elephant graveyard is a preordained site that animals voluntarily enter, the legend likely began as a way to explain the occasional discovery of large groupings of elephant carcasses. These have been found near water sources, where older and sickly elephants live and die in close proximity. Elephants are also quite susceptible to fatal malnutrition, which progresses quickly from extreme lethargy to death. When an entire herd is wiped out by drought or disease, the remaining bones are often found en masse at the herd's final watering hole.

There are other explanations for large collections of elephant bones. Pits of quicksand or bogs can trap a number of elephants; flash floods often wash all debris (not just elephant bones) from the valley floor into a common area; and poachers have been known to slay entire herds of elephants for their ivory, leaving the carcasses behind.

In parts of East Africa, however, groups of elephant corpses are thought to be the work of the *mazuku*, the Swahili word for "evil wind." Scientists have found volcanic vents in the earth's crust that emit carbon monoxide and other toxic gases. The noxious air released from these vents is forceful enough to blow out a candle's flame, and the remains of small mammals and birds are frequently found nearby. Humans and cattle have died as well. Although these vents have not proved to be powerful enough to kill groups of elephants, tales of the *mazuku* persist.

Although no longer considered a destination for elephants, the elephant graveyard still exists as a geologic term and as a figure of speech that refers to a repository of useless or outdated items. Given how prominent the legend remains in popular culture, it will be a long time before the elephant graveyard joins other such myths in a burial ground of its own.

Stuff about Sharks

⚓ Sharks have been around for nearly 400 million years. It's believed that larger, now extinct species used to eat dinosaurs.

⚓ Sharks have no tongues. Their taste buds are in their teeth.

⚓ Bull sharks, one of the most dangerous, aggressive shark species, have the highest testosterone levels of any animal in the world. They are also the only species of shark that can survive in both saltwater and freshwater.

⚓ Sharks are well known for their "sixth sense"—the ability to sense electromagnetic pulses sent out by creatures and objects in the water. The sensors in their snouts are small pores called the ampullae of Lorenzini.

⚓ Scientists have discovered that a shark can be put into a catatonic state called "tonic immobility" when it's flipped onto its back or when the ampullae of Lorenzini are appropriately stimulated. When the contact is stopped or the animal is righted, the shark typically snaps out of the "trance" very quickly.

⚓ Several types of sharks have demonstrated an affinity for being touched or for being put into a state of tonic immobility. Scientists have seen Caribbean reef sharks compete with each other for a diver's attention, sometimes ignoring food in favor of being touched. Some great whites have even shown positive responses to being touched and have allowed divers to ride along on their dorsal fins. (This is, of course, very dangerous even for professionals.)

🦆 Humans are significantly more dangerous to sharks than sharks are to humans. People kill as many as 100 million sharks every year, often when the sharks are accidentally caught in fishing nets. Many other sharks are caught only for their fins, which are cut off (to be used in shark-fin soup) before the still-living sharks are thrown back into the sea to drown.

🦆 The largest known shark litter was discovered in a blue shark. When examined, she carried 135 pups in her uterus.

🦆 Tiger sharks are often called the "garbage cans of the sea" because they will eat nearly anything. They favor sea turtles, but the contents of their stomachs have revealed tires, baseballs, and license plates.

🦆 Although short-fin mako sharks are renowned for their ability to jump out of the water, the great white shark also makes spectacular aerial breaches, particularly when hunting seals off the coast of South Africa. Occasionally, they land in passing boats, much to the surprise of passengers.

🦆 Sharks are not the mindless killers of lore. Many species have shown extraordinary curiosity and intelligence. They migrate to new feeding grounds at the times their prey is most plentiful there, and they adapt their hunting techniques depending on their prey. Some have even been trained to push a bell to receive food.

🦆 Great whites are frightening enough, but they have an extinct relative that makes the biggest of them look unimposing. *Carcharodon megalodon* was a huge shark that grew to 50 feet long and could easily swallow an entire person. They died out around a million years ago.

🦆 Short-finned makos are the fastest sharks out there. They have been clocked at 36 miles per hour and have been estimated to swim up to 60 miles per hour. They need this extreme speed to chase down their favorite food—the lightning-fast yellowfin tuna.

🦆 Most sharks are solitary hunters, but others are quite social. Greater hammerheads are known to group Into large schools of 100 or more off the Island of Cacos near Mexico, and blacktip reef sharks frequently hunt in packs the way wolves do, helping one another grab fish and crabs out of the coral.

🦆 Scientists have identified more than 400 species of sharks in the world, ranging from less than a foot long to 40-foot behemoths. Approximately 30 of those species are considered dangerous.

🦆 The pygmy ribbontail catshark is the smallest shark in the world, with a maximum length of seven inches.

🦆 Movies such as *Jaws* may make us think otherwise, but shark bites are uncommon, and fatal attacks rarely occur. A person is 1,000 times more likely to be bitten by a dog than by a shark, and dogs kill more people every year than sharks do.

🦆 If you happen to be attacked by a shark, try to gouge its eyes and gills, its most sensitive areas. Sharks are opportunistic feeders and generally don't pursue prey that puts up a fight in which they could be injured.

🦆 Gansbaii, South Africa, touts itself as the "Great White Capital of the World," and for good reason. Its shores host the greatest concentration of great white sharks in any ocean.

🦆 Great white attacks are usually caused by the animals' curiosity about an unfamiliar object. They are extremely curious, and lacking hands, they "feel out" the new object with their teeth, usually in a gentle bite. Unfortunately, the sharks are so large that even a nibble can do a lot of damage. The common belief that great white bites are a case of mistaken identity is false. Great whites have sharp eyesight, and they are often placid when interacting with humans— behavior that differs greatly when they are hunting seals.

The Weirdest Creature in the Sea

Sure, once you hit a certain depth, every sea creature is weird—there's the terrifying angler fish, famous for its appearance in the movie *Finding Nemo*; the purple jellyfish, which lights up the sea like a Chinese lantern; the horrid stonefish, with a face not even a mother could love; and the straight-out-of-science-fiction chimaera, or ghost shark, with its long snout and venomous dorsal spine. Yes, there are a lot of "weirdest creature" candidates down there, but one stands out even amid such strangeness.

Dracula of the Deep Sea

For the winner, we're going with one of the ocean's lesser-known oddities: the ominous vampire squid. The sole member of the order *Vampyromorphida*, the vampire squid's scientific name is *Vampyroteuthis infernalis*, which translates literally into "vampire squid from Hell." The squid is as black as night and has a pair of bloodshot eyes. Full-grown, it is no more than a foot long. For its size, it has the largest eyes of any animal in the world. Its ruby peepers are as large as a wolf's eyes, sometimes more than an inch in diameter.

All Lit Up

Like many deep-sea denizens, the vampire squid has bioluminescent photophores all over its body. The squid can apparently turn these lights on and off at will, and it uses this ability—combined with the blackness of its skin against the utter dark of the deep—to attract and disorient its prey.

The vampire squid is not a true squid—the order *Vampyromorphida* falls somewhere between the squid and the octopus—and does not possess an ink sac. In compensation, the vampire squid has the ability to expel a cloud of mucus when threatened; this mucus contains thousands of tiny bioluminescent orbs that serve to blind and confuse predators while the vampire squid escapes into the shadows. As a second deterrent to predators, the vampire squid can turn itself inside out, exposing its suckers and *cirri* (tiny hair-like growths that act as tactile sensors) and making the creature look as though it is covered with spines.

Despite its name, the vampire squid does not feed on blood; its diet consists mostly of prawns and other tiny, floating creatures. Other than that, all that's missing for this Béla Lugosi mimic are the fangs and the widow's peak. But before you reach for a wooden stake, you should know that the vampire squid poses absolutely no threat to humans. It's found mostly at 1,500 to 2,500 feet below the surface, so the odds of encountering one are pretty slim.

Mike the Headless Chicken

Chickens are known not for their intelligence but for their pecking, their much-emulated dance, and, in one special case, a chicken named Mike was known for losing his head.

A Slip of the Knife

On a fall day in 1945, on a farm in Fruita, Colorado, chickens were meeting their maker. It was nothing out of the ordinary; Lloyd and Clara Olsen slaughtered chickens on their farm all the time. But this particular day was fortuitous for Lloyd and one of his chickens. As Lloyd brought down his knife on the neck of a future meal, the head came off, clean as a whistle. The decapitated chicken flapped and danced around, which is what normally happens when a chicken loses its head.

But this chicken didn't stop flapping and dancing around. Most headless chickens only live a few minutes before going to that big chicken coop in the sky, but this particular bird was alive and well several hours (and then several months) after it had lost its, er, mind.

Open Mike

Lloyd was fascinated by this chicken that had somehow cheated death. The chicken continued to behave exactly like the other chickens on the farm—he just didn't have a head. Mike, as he was named, even attempted to cluck, although it sounded more like a gurgle since it came out of a hole in his neck.

Lloyd was starting to see the entrepreneurial possibilities that Mike had created—a living, breathing headless chicken was sure to be a goldmine. But Lloyd knew he had to devise a way for Mike to get nutrients or he would die. Using an eyedropper, a mixture of ground-up grain and water was sent down Mike's open esophagus, and little bits of gravel were dropped down his throat to help his gizzard grind up food.

That'll Be a Quarter

Mike the Headless Chicken was not some magical beast with the ability to cheat death; he was just an ordinary chicken that got lucky. Scientists who examined Mike determined that Lloyd had done a shoddy job of butchering him. Most of his head was actually gone, but the slice had missed Mike's jugular vein, and a blood clot prevented him from bleeding to death. Most of a chicken's reflex actions originate in the brain stem, and Mike's was pretty much untouched.

None of this mattered to the general public. When Mike went on a national sideshow tour in 1945, people lined up to see this wonder chicken and paid a quarter for the privilege. At his most popular, Mike was drawing in about $4,500 per month, which is equivalent to about $50,000 today. He was insured for $10,000 and featured in *Life* magazine. What became of Mike's head is a mystery. Most photos show a chicken head alongside Mike, either at his feet or pickled in a jar. But rumor has it that the Olsens' cat ate the original head, and Lloyd used another chicken's head as a stand-in.

A Moment of Silence, Please

It's wasn't the lack of a head that was toughest on Mike—he had a problem with choking on his own mucus. The Olsens used a syringe to suck it out of Mike's neck, but one night, Mike was traveling back home, roosting with the Olsens in their motel room. Lloyd and Clara heard Mike choking in the middle of the night. Alas, they discovered they had left the syringe in the last town where Mike had appeared. Mike succumbed to death that night in Phoenix in 1947. These days, Fruita holds a Mike the Headless Chicken Day every third weekend in May.

The Fate of the Passenger Pigeon

When Europeans first visited North America, the passenger pigeon was easily the most numerous bird on the entire continent. But by the early 1900s, the passenger pigeon was extinct. What led to this incredible change in fortune?

Pigeons on the Wing

From the first written description of the passenger pigeon in 1534, eyewitnesses struggled with how to describe what they saw. Flights of the 16-inch-long birds were staggeringly, almost mind-numbingly big; flocks were measured in the millions, if not billions, and could be heard coming for miles. When passing overhead, a flight could block out the sun to the point that chickens would come in to roost. Passenger pigeons flew at around 60 miles an hour—one nickname dubbed the bird the "blue meteor"—but even so, a group sighted by Cotton Mather was a mile long and took hours to pass overhead. At least one explorer hesitated to detail what he had seen, for fear that the entirety of his report would be dismissed as mere exaggeration.

Settlers viewed the pigeons with trepidation. A passing flock could wreak havoc on crops, stripping fields bare and leading to famine. A flight passing overhead or roosting on your land would leave everything covered with noxious bird droppings—a situation that would lead to more fertile soil in following years but did little to endear the creatures to farmers at that moment. In later years, naturalist Aldo Leopold would describe migrating passenger pigeons as "a biological storm." John James Audubon more bluntly referred to their droppings falling "like snow flakes."

Pigeons on the Table

With such vast numbers, what could possibly have led to the extinction of the passenger pigeon? There are a number of theories, but the most likely answer seems to be the most obvious: People hunted them out of existence. Native Americans had long used the pigeons as a food source, and the Europeans followed suit, developing a systematic approach to harvesting the birds that simply outstripped their ability to reproduce. At first, the practice was an exercise in survival—a case of explorers feeding themselves on the frontier or settlers eating pigeon meat in place of the crops the birds had destroyed. However, necessity soon evolved into a matter of convenience and simple economy—the birds were cheap to put on the table.

Killing the birds in bulk was almost a trivial exercise. Initially, settlers could walk up under trees of nesting birds and simply knock them down using oars. As the birds became more wary, firearms were a natural choice for hunters; flocks were so dense, one report gives an unbelievable count of 132 birds blasted out of the sky with a single shot. Nets were strung across fields, easily yanking the birds from the air as they flew. Perhaps most infamously, a captive bird would be tied to a small platform that was raised and then suddenly dropped; as the pigeon fluttered to the ground, other pigeons would think the decoy was alighting to feed and would fly down to join him—a practice that became the origin for the English term "stool pigeon." Hunters would catch the birds in nets, then kill them by crushing their heads between thumb and forefinger.

Pigeons on Display

By 1860, flocks had declined noticeably, and by the 1890s calls went out for a moratorium on hunting the animals—but to no avail. Conservation experts tried breeding the birds in captivity to little effect; it seemed the pigeons longed for the company of their enormous flocks and could not reproduce reliably without them. By the time experts realized this, the flocks no longer existed.

Sightings of passenger pigeons in the wild stopped by the early 1900s. A few survivors remained in captivity, dying one by one as ornithologists looked on helplessly. The last surviving pigeon, a female named Martha, died at the Cincinnati Zoological Garden on September 1, 1914. Her body was frozen in ice and shipped to the Smithsonian Institution, a testament to the downfall of a species.

10 Things to Do if You've Been Skunked

Skunks have it pretty rough. Their small size makes them prey for scores of large predators. They're scavengers, which means lunch is literally garbage, and many of them end up as roadkill. Read on to learn about how to avoid the path of a disgruntled skunk and what to do if you do tangle with one.

1. Stay Away: The best way to avoid getting skunked is to stay away from them. Skunks only spray when they're threatened, so don't threaten them and you shouldn't have a problem.

2. Speak Softly and Walk with a Big Stomp: If you must approach a skunk, do so with caution. Speak in a low voice and stomp your feet. Skunks have poor vision and often spray in defense because they simply don't know what's going on.

3. Freeze: Another tactic for avoiding a skunking is to stand perfectly still and wait for the skunk to go away. Passive, but effective.

4. Run . . . or Shut Your Eyes and Hang on Tight: Right before a skunk lets loose its spray of stinkiness, it stomps its feet and turns around, as the spray glands are located near the anus. If you see a skunk doing this little dance, run away or hang on tight, because you're about to get skunked.

5. Flush It Out: If you get sprayed in the face, immediately flush your face and eyes with water. The sulfur-alcohol compound that skunks emit can cause temporary blindness, which could lead to bigger problems.

6. Take It Outside: Now that you've been skunked, anything you come into contact with is going to smell like you do. You smell like skunk, if you hadn't already noticed. So try to stay outside, if at all possible.

7. Skip the V8, Air Freshener, and Lemon Juice: No matter what Grandma said, tomato juice does not take the smell of skunk off of you, your dog, or your clothes. And unless you like "fresh morning dew" skunk, vanilla skunk, or lemony skunk, don't even bother with air fresheners or lemon juice. These products don't eliminate skunk smell, they only make it worse by coating it with another cloying scent.

8. Mix Up a Peroxide Bath: To get rid of the skunk smell, you must neutralize the chemicals in the spray. This home remedy seems to work well on animals or humans: Mix one quart of 3 percent hydrogen peroxide, one teaspoon mild dishwashing detergent, and 1/4 cup baking soda in a bucket. Lather, rinse, repeat.

9. Buy Deodorizing Spray: These special sprays are available at pet stores and some home and garden stores, too. They work well because they're specially formulated to neutralize the intense odor of skunk.

10. Call the Public Health Department or Your Doctor: . . . if you've been bitten. Skunks have been known to carry rabies, even though they rarely resort to biting. The same goes for your pet—get it to the vet quickly if the skunk did more than spray. Also, notify the public health department within 24 hours.

Do Cows Cause Global Warming?

At first glance, cows embody the ideal for a clean, healthy planet. What could be better than a farmer working the land and raising animals in a lush, green meadow? But what's that sound? And—whoa!—that smell?

In addition to milk, meat, and leather, cows give us burps, farts, manure . . . and, in turn, methane. A cow has a four-chambered stomach. Food is partially digested in the first two chambers and then regurgitated for cud-chewing; the food is then fully digested in the third and fourth chambers. The food ferments as it is digested, and the gases expelled during this process (from either end of the cow) include methane. Even the "cow patties" the animal produces contain methane.

Of the greenhouse gases blamed for global warming, only carbon dioxide is considered more harmful than methane—carbon dioxide gets top billing because of the sheer volume of it floating around the atmosphere and trapping the sun's heat. Methane is at least twenty times better at trapping heat than carbon dioxide, and the volume of it that's in the atmosphere has almost doubled in the past two centuries. This, however, can't be blamed solely on cattle—landfills, decomposition in wetlands, coal mining, petroleum drilling, and even rice paddies produce large amounts of methane, as well.

Nevertheless, farm animals are definitely doing their share. Globally, about 15 or 20 percent of methane comes from livestock, including the world's more than one billion cows. Each of these cows has the potential to fill about three hundred two-liter bottles with gas each day. Once the methane produced by other four-stomached, or ruminant, livestock—including sheep, goats, and buffalo—is factored in, the annual global total is eighty million metric tons. This makes livestock one of the largest human-related sources of methane (as we're the ones feeding and raising them). In the United States alone, livestock account for about 20 percent of the methane released into the air.

Cows aren't going away anytime soon, so resourceful farmers and scientists are looking for ways to minimize the problem. For instance, improved nutrition for cows—feeding them more easily digestible grasses, for example—can help diminish their methane excretion. Scientists are also developing a new strain of grass that may further reduce cows' propensity toward toxic emissions.

In the meantime, the methane trapped in cows' solid waste is easy to harness and use productively. Methane is quite similar to the natural gas used for fuel, so some farms have taken to collecting cow poop, extracting the methane, and burning the gas to create electricity. As an added bonus, the remaining components of the manure can be used as fertilizer (the liquid) and as compost or even bedding (the dry remnants) for the very cattle that produced it.

Animals by the Bunch

Everyone is familiar with the saying "It's more fun than a barrel of monkeys." But how many times have you heard, "You're as loud as a murder of magpies" or "That's as smart as a wisdom of wombats"? Here are the official collective names for various groups of critters.

a congregation of alligators	a business of ferrets
a shoal of bass	a wisdom of wombats
a smack of jellyfish	a flamboyance of flamingoes
a gaze of raccoons	a rhumba of rattlesnakes
a clowder of cats	a gang of elk
a cackle of hyenas	a tower of giraffes
a troop of kangaroos	a tribe of goats
a leap of leopards	a band of gorillas
a fall of woodcocks	a bloat of hippopotamuses
a romp of otters	a richness of martens
a prickle of porcupines	a labor of moles
a crash of rhinoceroses	a pod of seals
a troubling of goldfish	a drove of sheep
a pod of whales	a dray of squirrels
a charm of finches	an ambush of tigers
an exaltation of larks	a wake of buzzards
a murder of magpies	a chain of bobolinks
a watch of nightingales	a gulp of cormorants
a parliament of owls	a convocation of eagles
a covey of partridges	a sedge of herons
an ostentation of peacocks	a party of jays
a colony of penguins	a deceit of lapwings
a bevy of quails	a murder of ravens

When Alligators Look for Low, Low Prices

These days in Florida, alligators don't just wander across golf courses on their way to the swamp. In 2013, a six-foot-long alligator waddled up to the door of a Walmart and proceeded to loiter there for an hour. The reptile seemed calm—"just chilling," as one customer reported. Alligators are also becoming increasingly unafraid of suburban neighborhoods. In 2008, a 230-pound female alligator broke through a screened door and made its way into a woman's kitchen, where it proceeded to break some dishes and terrorize the house cat (the cat was unharmed, but now prefers the second floor). But probably one of the most alarming instances of alligator trespass occurred in 2016, when an alligator was caught on video trudging up the sidewalk of a private residence and getting up on its hind legs in what looked like an attempt to ring the doorbell repeatedly.

CHAPTER 3

In Either 1492 or 1776 Napoleon Signed the Magna Carta

History is filled with dates. A wise man once said, "the problem with dates is that there are so many numbers." Well, maybe not a wise man, but the point is that if it weren't for dates and facts, history would be a lot less tedious and your grade point average would have been higher in high school.

History as a subject should be pretty simple. It's all about events: wars, treaties, arrivals, departures, more wars . . . tough to mess that up, right? Napoleon, on the other hand, believed that history is "a set of lies that people have agreed upon." He spoke from experience: he owned several European newspapers and sometimes penned his own accounts of military events, once assuring his readers that "Bonaparte flies like lightning and strikes like a thunderbolt."

Napoleon's main adversary was savvy to the method. They were also familiar with the related saying, "history is written by the victors." Remember that bit of "history" about Napoleon being really, really short? He wasn't. That was a myth invented by the English.

1492: The Year Columbus Stuck to His Story

Columbus Day is a holiday that honors the fact that Columbus discovered America. But according to the historians—and Columbus himself—he missed the mark. Yes, he did cross the Atlantic in 1492. He was convinced he could find a route to the Far East (or "the Indies") that wouldn't require him to sail all the way around the Horn of Africa. On October 12, he landed on a small body of land, believing it was one of the outlying islands of the fabled Orient. Today, we celebrate Columbus Day and continue to give props to Columbus for his "discovery."

The truth is that Columbus first landed somewhere in the Bahamas—there is some disagreement as to exactly which island he set foot on—and from there went on to Cuba (he thought it was China) and Hispaniola (present-day Haiti and the Dominican Republic, which he thought was Japan). During his second trip, Columbus returned to Hispaniola, and it wasn't until his third voyage that he finally landed in America—South America, that is, in what is now Venezuela.

Columbus wrote, "For the execution of the voyage to the Indies, I did not make use of intelligence, mathematics, or maps." This explains a lot.

Columbus made one last voyage across the Atlantic in 1502, hoping for definitive proof that he'd found a western route to the Indies. Instead, he discovered St. Lucia, Honduras, Costa Rica, and the Isthmus of Panama.

By that time, another Italian mariner, Amerigo Vespucci, had sailed along the coast of South America and proposed that it was not Asia at all but an entirely new continent.

Columbus was nothing if not resolute. He continued to insist that he had discovered a new route to the Indies until the day he died in 1506. A year later, a German mapmaker included the new-found lands on a world map and called them America, in honor of Vespucci. It was the first time the name had been used. Columbus wasn't around to complain, and the name stuck.

The Tell on William Tell

Most of us imbibed the legend as children and most of us probably still believe it really happened. But did it? Let's go over the details again. In 1307, Austria's Hapsburgs wanted to clamp down on the Swiss. An Austrian official named Hermann Gessler put his hat atop a pole and then made a petty, ridiculous rule: All passersby had to bow to his hat. An expert crossbowman named William Tell refused to bow, so Gessler's police arrested him. But Gessler wasn't satisfied with that.

In a fit of sadistic temper, Gessler made a deal with Tell. If Tell could shoot an apple off Tell's son's head with the crossbow, both would be free. If Tell whiffed, or nailed his son, Gessler would execute him. Tell hit the apple but couldn't resist a snarky comment to Gessler. The latter, not renowned for his joie de vivre, got mad and threw Tell in jail. Eventually, Tell escaped and assassinated Gessler. This touched off a rebellion that led to the Swiss Confederation (still in business today, operating banks and ski lifts).

Where's the controversy? To begin with, there is no con-temporary historical evidence for Tell or Gessler. The legend first appeared in the late 1400s, and no one can explain the delay. What's more, the motif of an archer shooting a target off his son's head, then slaying a tyrant, appears in diverse Germanic literature predating 1307. It's not that the William Tell legend is necessarily false, because we can't prove it. The combination of faults—lack of evidence, duplication of older legends—makes the legend a tough sell as history.

How do the Swiss feel about it? It wasn't easy for Swiss patriots to carve out and hold their own country with all the warlike tides of Europe buffeting them. The multilingual Swiss have built and maintained a prosperous Confedera-tion that avoids warfare from a position of strength. Wil-liam Tell symbolizes Swiss love of freedom and disdain for tyrants, domestic or foreign.

The News Is What the President Says It Is

Politicians often cite the actions of their historical forebears to justify their own indiscretions. Abraham Lincoln, for example, is said to have suppressed civil rights during the Civil War, so he occasionally gets referenced when a mod-ern politician wants to do the same thing. Today's official might say, "Lincoln suppressed newspapers during the Civil War, so I should be able to meddle with a few civil liberties, too." But did Lincoln really work to curtail freedom of the press? It's not quite so clear cut.

Freedom of the Press?

A handful of cases are frequently cited to portray Lincoln as opposed to a free press. In June 1863, the editor of the *Chicago Times* wrote inflammatory antiwar articles that attacked the efforts of Lincoln and the Republicans. Union General Ambrose Burnside, who was in command of the Department of the Ohio at the time, was alarmed at what he considered the *Times*'s "repeated expression of disloyal and incendiary sentiments." The general had the editor arrested and the paper shut down. Although Lincoln had suspended habeas corpus in areas where he feared physical unrest, he was troubled by Burnside's actions and consulted his Cabinet for a response. They agreed that the editor's arrest had been improper, so Lincoln freed him and allowed the *Chicago Times* to return to press. When people asked Lincoln why he hadn't supported the closure of the newspaper that had been so critical of him, he wrote that those with such a question did "not fully comprehend the dangers of abridging the liberties of the people." That doesn't sound like something a hater of the press would write!

Lies Instead of News

The President wasn't completely above shutting down a printing press if he thought it was necessary. On May 18, 1864, the *New York World* and the *Journal of Commerce* each published a forged presidential proclamation calling for a new draft of 400,000 troops. Once these papers were on the street, the administration wasted no time in going after them. Lincoln himself ordered General John A. Dix to arrest the publishers and editors and to seize their presses. When further investigation determined that the journalists had been taken in by the forgery themselves and had never intended to convey false information, the journalists were released and allowed to resume publication.

In his telegram to Dix releasing the journalists, Secretary of War Edwin Stanton wrote of the President, "He directs me to say that while, in his opinion, the editors, proprietors, and publishers of *The World* and *Journal of Commerce* are responsible for what appears in their papers injurious to the public service, and have no right to shield themselves behind a plea of ignorance or want of criminal intent, yet he is not disposed to visit them with vindictive punishment."

The People Have Spoken

Official action from the government wasn't the only sort of suppression that affected newspapers. In March 1863, the 2nd Ohio Cavalry was camped outside of Columbus, Ohio. After the local newspaper, *The Crisis*, printed anti-army stories—including the wish that no member of the 2nd Ohio return from the war alive—the soldiers ransacked its offices. *The Crisis* continued publication, however. The next year, its editor was indicted by a federal grand jury and arrested for conspiracy. He died in November before he could go on trial.

Although Lincoln wasn't afraid to take action when he felt it necessary, he was keenly aware of the danger in restricting civil rights and did so only after careful consideration. Those wishing to use him as a role model for their actions against free speech should perhaps take a closer look.

Cleopatra: Stranger than Fiction

In his work, *Antony and Cleopatra*, the immortal William Shakespeare gave Egypt's most famous queen the following line: "Be it known that we, the greatest, are misthought." These "misthoughts" could be the myths, embellishments, untruths, and fallacies that seem to surround Cleopatra.

Though movies and the media tend to focus on these misconceptions, the true stories are equally fascinating.

MYTH: Cleopatra was Egyptian.
FACT: Cleopatra may have been the queen of Egypt, but she was actually Greek. Though her family had called Egypt home for hundreds of years, their lineage was linked to a general in Alexander the Great's army named Ptolemy who had come from Macedonia, an area in present-day Greece.

MYTH: Cleopatra was a vision of beauty.
FACT: Beauty, of course, is in the eye of the beholder. In ancient times, there were no cameras, but a person of Cleopatra's stature and wealth could have their likeness sculpted. If the image on an ancient Roman coin is believed to be accurate, then Cleopatra was endowed with a large, hooked nose and was as cheeky as a chipmunk.

MYTH: Cleopatra dissolved a pearl earring in a glass of vinegar and drank it. As the story goes, upon meeting Marc Antony, Cleopatra held a series of lavish feasts. On the eve of the final gala, Cleopatra bet Antony that she could arrange for the costliest meal in the world. As the banquet came to a close, she supposedly removed an enormous pearl from her ear, dropped it into a goblet of wine vinegar, then drank it down, with Antony admitting defeat.
FACT: Scientifically speaking, calcium carbonate—the mineral of which pearls are composed—will dissolve in an acid such as vinegar. However, based on the description of the pearl in question, it is likely that the short dip in vinegar resulted in nothing more than a soggy gem, as it would have taken a very long time for that amount of calcium carbonate to dissolve.

MYTH: Julius Caesar allowed Cleopatra to remain queen of Egypt because he loved her.

FACT: Though not married, Cleopatra did bear Caesar a son, whose name was Caesarion. However, that was hardly reason enough to hand over an entire country to her. Most likely, Caesar felt that any male ruler would pose a formidable threat to his empire, whereas Cleopatra was a safer alternative to rule Egypt.

MYTH: Cleopatra died from the bite of an asp after learning of Marc Antony's death.

FACT: It's unknown exactly how or why Cleopatra decided to take her own life. According to legend, after hearing of the death of her lover, she had two poisonous asps brought to her concealed in a basket of figs. The person who found the expired Cleopatra noted two small marks on her arm, but the snakes in question were never located. Cleopatra may very well have been distraught about her lover's demise, but it is more likely that rumors she was about to be captured, chained, and exhibited in the streets of Rome drove her to suicide.

It's Not True, by George!

George Washington is known for a great many things, some of which are true (he was the only president to be elected unanimously) and many others that are imagined. Here are three of the latter.

He Wore Wooden Dentures

It's common knowledge that Washington had gnawing dental problems. This brought the leader much pain and sent him in search of any relief he could find. Over time, each of Washington's teeth had to be extracted and replaced with dentures. Legend holds that these dental appliances were fashioned from wood, which (some say) could account for Washington's "wooden" smile.

In fact, Washington's false teeth were made from both hippopotamus and elephant ivory, as well as human teeth that were not his own. During his lifetime, Washington used several sets of falsies. Most were ill-fitting and therefore contorted his expression, but none were made from wood.

He Threw a Silver Dollar across the Potomac

George was a tall (6'2"), athletic man, but he certainly wasn't a good enough throw to hurl a silver dollar all the way across the Potomac River, which is close to a mile wide at Mount Vernon, Maryland (site of the president's home).

There is evidence that, as a boy, he tossed something across the Rappahannock River in Fredericksburg, Virginia (near his childhood home). If that's the case, though, that "something" certainly wasn't a silver dollar, because the coins didn't even exist when Washington was young.

He Wore a Wig

Despite the fact that it was all the rage for men to sport a powdery hair helmet in the late 1700s, George would go only so far to fit in. He kept his brownish-red hair at a length that allowed him to tie it back in a braid, and then he'd occasionally give it a good dusting of powder just for the sake of fashion.

Lies about Pilgrims

FALLACY: Pilgrims left England for America because of religious persecution.

FACT: Then called Separatists, the Pilgrims did leave England to escape religious persecution. However, they first went to Leiden in the Netherlands, not the wilderness of America. After a few years in Leiden, the Separatists grew discontented at the bottom of the commerce-driven Dutch totem pole. Worse still, their children were learning liberal Dutch ideas, including religious tolerance. To keep Satan from gaining a victory through the children, and to preserve English identity, the Separatists decided to leave.

FALLACY: Going to (future) Massachusetts was a foregone conclusion for the Pilgrims.

FACT: They first considered Guiana (where the Dutch had already established a colony called Essequibo) and the existing settlements in Virginia.

FALLACY: They sought religious freedom in America.

FACT: Not as most Americans understand it today. By "religious freedom," Pilgrims meant freedom to be a Pilgrim, not something other than a Pilgrim. Native Americans and Quakers would discover that the fine print didn't include a cheerful embrace of pluralistic religious beliefs.

FALLACY: Most of the *Mayflower* passengers were Pilgrims.

FACT: About half were. It's easy to forget now that the Mayflower voyage was in essence a commercial venture, with the Separatists/Pilgrims as homesteaders and cheap labor. The backers jacked the Separatists around, breaking various promises. The secular passengers—who would cause some trouble in the New World—were mostly fortune-seekers completely uninterested in a devout lifestyle.

FALLACY: The Pilgrims first landed at Plymouth.
FACT: No, they made their first landfall at Provincetown on Cape Cod after a perilous approach. It didn't take the Pilgrims long to see that Provincetown made a crummy site for a colony.

FALLACY: Pocahontas, John Smith, and Powhatan were key figures in Pilgrim history.
FACT: Don't confuse the colonies: Jamestown (Virginia, 1607) and Plymouth (Massachusetts, 1620) were dissimilar settlements, with little direct contact. John Smith, the Native American princess Pocahontas, and her father Powhatan all figure in the Jamestown story. Miles Standish, Squanto, and Massasoit (leader of the Pokanoket) are part of the Plymouth/Pilgrim saga.

FALLACY: Pilgrims were essentially Puritans.
FACT: Not at first. The key theological difference between them was their relationship to the Anglican Church. Puritans wanted to reform the Church, Pilgrims abandoned it. However, when the Puritans began to follow the Pilgrims to New England, Puritanism essentially engulfed and absorbed its more tolerant Separatist brethren.

FALLACY: The Pilgrims immediately began stealing Indian land.
FACT: This isn't even possible. The tribes of the region had already been depleted by a staggering 90 percent because of disease, yet even that hardy, tragic remnant vastly outnumbered the initial *Mayflower* colonists. Thus, the Indian survivors had plenty of land to sell (or trade for flintlock muskets). Most Pilgrim leaders made successful efforts to get along with their Indian neighbors—probably more out of pragmatism than love of diversity. Any other course would have been self-destructive.

Babe Ruth's Called Shot

Did Ruth call a home run in the 1932 World Series? This much is known: the Yankees had already won the first two games of the '32 fall classic when they met the Cubs at Wrigley Field for Game 3. Although Chicago players were understandably frustrated, there was bad blood between the teams that extended beyond the norm. In August, the Cubs had picked up former Yankee shortstop Mark Koenig from the Pacific Coast League to replace injured starter Billy Jurges, and Koenig hit .353 the rest of the season. Despite these heroics, his new teammates had only voted him a half-share of their World Series bonus money—a slight that enraged his old colleagues. The Yanks engaged in furious bench-jockeying with their "cheapskate" opponents the entire series, and Chicago players and fans shouted back, jeering that Ruth was old, fat, and washed-up.

Up to Bat

When Ruth stepped up to bat in the fifth inning of Game 3, the taunts started as usual. A few people threw lemons at Babe from the stands, and he gestured toward the crowd before settling in at the plate. Charlie Root's first pitch was a called strike, and Ruth, looking over at the Chicago dugout, appeared to hold up one finger—as if to say, "That's only one." He did the same thing with two fingers after taking the second pitch, another strike. Then, some eyewitnesses recalled, he pointed toward dead center field. Others didn't remember this act, but there was no mistaking what happened next: Ruth slammed Root's third offering deep into the edge of the right-field bleachers. Onlookers recalled him laughing as he rounded the bases. And, as shown in a much-published photo, he and on-deck batter Lou Gehrig laughed and shook hands back at home plate.

What Really Happened?

Here is where the facts end and speculation begins. Those among the 49,986 fans on hand who noticed Ruth's display likely assumed it was just another round in the ongoing feud between the two clubs, and most sportswriters made nothing out of it in their accounts of New York's 7–5 victory. The homer was not a game-winner; it was just one (in fact, the last) of 15 home runs Ruth hit in World Series play during his career. He had already taken Root deep earlier in the same contest, and Gehrig also had two in the game. The Yanks finished their four-game sweep the next day.

This being Babe Ruth, however, it only took a few speculative accounts from among the many reporters present to get the ball rolling. "Ruth Calls Shot" read the headline in the next day's *New York World Telegram*, and soon sports fans everywhere were wondering. Gehrig claimed he heard Ruth yell to Root, "I'm going to knock the next one down your goddamned throat" before the fateful pitch, while Cubs catcher Gabby Hartnett recalled the remark as "It only takes one to hit." Root and Cubs second baseman Billy Herman denied any gesture to the outfield, and grainy film footage that surfaced in 1999 was unclear either way. Ever the diplomat, Ruth himself granted some interviews in which he substanti-

ated the claim, and others in which he denied it. So did he or didn't he? We may never know for sure, but perhaps it's better that way. When the subject is Babe Ruth, facts are only half the fun.

Wrong, Wrong, Wrong

Here are some classic cases of the history books getting it totally wrong—in some cases for centuries. Some of these tales were originally based on fact, but all became twisted and embellished as they were told and retold like a game of telephone.

Lady Godiva's Naked Ride

Even if the Internet had existed during the Middle Ages, you wouldn't have been able to download nude pictures of Lady Godiva because she never actually rode naked through the streets of Coventry, England. Godiva was a real person who lived in the 11th century and she really did plead with her ruthless husband, Leofric, the Earl of Mercia, to reduce taxes. But no records of the time mention her famous ride. The first reference to her naked ride doesn't appear until around 1236, nearly 200 years after her death.

Sir Walter Raleigh's Cloak

The story goes that Sir Walter Raleigh laid his cloak over a mud puddle to keep Queen Elizabeth I from getting her feet wet. Raleigh did catch the queen's attention in 1581 when he urged England to conquer Ireland. The queen rewarded him with extensive landholdings in England and Ireland, knighted him in 1584, and named him captain of the queen's guard two years later. But an illicit affair with one of the queen's maids of honor in 1592 did him in. He was imprisoned in the Tower of London and ultimately beheaded for treachery. The story of the cloak and the mud puddle probably originated with historian Thomas Fuller, who was known for embellishing facts.

Nero Fiddled While Rome Burned

When asked who fiddled while Rome burned, the answer "Nero" will get you a zero. Legend has it that in AD 64, mad Emperor Nero started a fire near the imperial palace and then climbed to the top of the Tower of Maecenas where he played his fiddle, sang arias, and watched Rome flame out. But according to Tacitus, a historian of the time, Nero was 30 miles away, at his villa in Antium, when the fire broke out. Nero wasn't exactly a nice guy—he took his own mother as his mistress, then had her put to death. Despite this, historians believe that the fire was set by Nero's political enemies, who were right in thinking that it would be blamed on him. Actually, Nero was a hero, attempting to extinguish the blaze, finding food and shelter for the homeless, and overseeing the design of the new city.

The Forbidden Fruit

Both the apple and Eve get an undeserved bad rap in the story of Paradise. According to the Book of Genesis, Adam and Eve were evicted from Paradise for eating "the fruit of the tree which is in the midst of the garden." There's no mention of any apple! Some biblical scholars think it was a fig, since Adam and Eve dressed in fig leaves, while Muslim scholars think it may have been wheat or possibly grapes. Aquila Ponticus, a 2nd-century translator of the Old Testament, may have assumed that the apple tree in the Song of Solomon was the fruit-bearing tree in Genesis. Two centuries later, St. Jerome also linked the apple tree to the phrase "there wast thou corrupted" in his Latin translation of the Old Testament.

Cinderella Wore Glass Slippers

Ask anyone and they'll tell you that Cinderella wore glass slippers to the ball, but historians say that part of the legend isn't true. More than 500 versions of the classic fairy tale exist, dating back as far as the 9th century. In each account, Cinderella has a magic ring or magic slippers made of gold, silver, or some other rare metal, which are sometimes covered with gems but are never made of glass. In the earliest French versions, Cinderella wore *pantoufles en vair* or "slippers of white squirrel fur." In 1697, when French writer Charles Perrault wrote "Cendrillon," his version of the tale, the word vair had vanished from the French language. Perrault apparently assumed it should have been verre, pronounced the same as vair, but meaning "glass." Even a wave of the fairy godmother's magic wand couldn't make that mistake disappear, and it has been passed down ever since.

Witches Were Burned at the Stake in Salem

Although there really were witch trials in Salem, Massachusetts, in 1692, and 20 people were put to death, none of the accused were burned at the stake. Hanging was the preferred method of execution, although one victim was crushed to death under heavy stones. Moreover, there's no evidence these people were practicing witchcraft or were possessed by the devil. Historians now believe that they, along with the townspeople who persecuted them, were suffering from mass hysteria. Others believe the accusers were afflicted with a physical illness, possibly even hallucinating after eating tainted rye bread.

"Let Them Eat Cake"

She probably said a lot of things she later regretted, but Marie Antoinette never suggested French mothers who had no bread should eat cake. In 1766, Jean Jacques Rousseau was writing his "Confessions" when he quoted the famous saying of a great princess, which was incorrectly attributed to Marie Antoinette, Queen of France and wife of Louis XVI. But Marie Antoinette couldn't have made the statement because in 1766, she was only 11 years old. Historians now believe that Rousseau's "great princess" may have been Marie Thérèse, the wife of Louis XIV, who reigned more than 75 years before Louis XVI and Marie Antoinette.

The Great Wall of China Is Visible from the Moon

You can see a lot of things while standing on the moon, but the Great Wall of China isn't one of them. In his 1938 publication, *Second Book of Marvels*, Richard Halliburton stated that the Great Wall was the only human-made object visible from the moon. However, the Great Wall is only a maximum of 30 feet wide and is about the same color as its surroundings, so it's barely visible to the naked eye while orbiting Earth under ideal conditions, much less from the moon, which is about 239,000 miles away.

Ben Franklin Discovered Electricity

Benjamin Franklin did not discover electricity when his kite was struck by lightning in 1752. In fact, electricity was already well known at the time. Instead, Franklin was trying to prove the electrical nature of lightning. During a thunderstorm, as Franklin flew a silk kite with a metal key near the end of the string, he noticed the fibers on the line standing up as though charged. He touched the key and felt a charge from the accumulated electricity in the air, not from a lightning strike. This was enough evidence to prove his theory that lightning was electricity. Had the kite been struck by lightning, Franklin would likely have been killed as was Professor Georg Wilhelm Richmann of St. Petersburg, Russia, when he attempted the same experiment a few months later.

Steel-Driving John Henry

"But John Henry drove his steel sixteen feet . . . an' the steam drill drove only nine." So the song goes. We'd like to believe in John Henry. Two different towns claim him, but who's right?

Retelling the Legend

It's a great one. They say that John Henry was born and raised a slave, perhaps in the 1840s. He grew up into a fortress of a man, a mighty worker, and after slavery ended he went to work for a railroad. In order to blast railroad tunnels, someone had to hammer a long steel stake deep into the rock, creating a hole where others could slide in dynamite. After workers cleared away the blasted rock, the "steel-driving men" got busy pounding more stakes. Henry was the best in the business. One day someone brought in a newfangled steam drill or steam hammer, probably suggesting in scornful tones that Henry's skill was now obsolete. John challenged the steam drill to a contest, outdrove it almost two to one, then keeled over from a heart attack.

The trouble with that story? It's a lack of evidence or conflicting evidence. No one doubts that a mighty ex-slave worked on railroad-construction gangs; many thousands of freedmen did, and it wasn't a job for the weak. It's plausible that one such man, full of heart and pride, challenged a steam drill and lost. But where and when did this happen? "John Henry" was a common enough name, appearing often in railroad employment records. Different accounts, none well corroborated, place the event in different states. If big John lived, it's unfortunate for his memory that people didn't bother keeping detailed records. But we can't make the story true by wishing it so.

Where does this scant evidence place John? Some believe that the steam drill challenge occurred at Talcott, West Virginia. Others place it near Leeds, Alabama. One historian argues that Henry was a prisoner leased out by the warden (a legal practice in those days). We don't know for sure, though both towns commemorate John Henry. All of the claims can't be right; possibly none are.

So we can say nothing with authority? Actually, we can say a great deal. John Henry, fictional or real, reminds us of much undisputed history and human nature. Any person, even if illiterate and raised in slavery, has personal pride that should never be laughed away. For many, and especially freedmen, manual labor paid ridiculously low wages for dangerous, difficult work. As the 20th century approached, machines took over more and more jobs. A man with a hammer, defying the boss and his job-stealing machine, is an evocative symbol of labor. And whether he lived or not, John Henry represents the mighty part played by every African-American cowhand, rail worker, blacksmith, home-maker, and millhand as the United States expanded west. That's worth remembering.

Gene Siskel's Last Thumb

Few in the specialized field of film criticism have been as well known or respected as Gene Siskel, who penned countless movie reviews for the *Chicago Tribune* and later teamed up with fellow critic Roger Ebert of the *Chicago Sun-Times* on the popular television show *At the Movies*.

The show was famous for its movie rating system of "thumbs up–thumbs down," which became the duo's critical trademark. Shortly after Siskel's death in 1999 from complications following brain surgery, a story started to circulate that, among other provisions, Siskel's will stipulated that he be buried with his thumb pointing skyward. Siskel's thumbs had made him internationally renowned, a legacy that he may have wanted to take to his grave. The rumor raced through the Internet in the form of a fake UPI news story that noted Siskel's unusual request. It read, in part: "According to public records filed in chancery court in Chicago, Gene Siskel asked that he be buried with his thumb pointing upward. The 'Thumbs Up' was the Siskel–Ebert trademark."

The story continued: "'Gene wanted to be remembered as a thumbs-up kind of guy,' said Siskel's lawyer. 'It wasn't surprising to me that he'd ask for that. I informed his family after his death, but he didn't want it made public until after his will had been read.'" The faux article carries all of the marks of a typical urban legend. Most telling is its failure to identify Siskel's attorney by name, an omission that no legitimate news organization would make.

The magazine *Time Out New York* investigated the rumor and set the record straight, reporting on July 15, 1999: "A glance at the will, now on file with a Chicago court, makes clear that there are no digit-placement requests in [Siskel's] last wishes."

The Long Shadow of the Ninja

Ninjas were the special forces of feudal Japan. Trained in assassination, espionage, and guerilla warfare, ninjas inspired fear in both rulers and commoners alike. Over the years, the ninja has taken on a mythical status. But like most myths, the story is filled with both fact and fiction.

Humble Beginnings

Ninjas got their start as priests living in the mountains of Japan. Harassed by the central government and local samurai, they resorted to using *Nonuse* (the art of stealth)—what we would call guerilla warfare. Their use of secrecy and stealth didn't win them many friends, but it secured them a role in the civil wars to come.

From roughly 794 to 1192, local rulers fought to gain control of Japan. While the Samurai fought the wars, it was left to the mountain priests to do those things that the Samurai considered cowardly—namely spying, sneaking around to gather information, and trying to assassinate their rivals. This is when the ninja (*nin*, meaning "concealment" and *sha*, meaning "person") was born.

From Priests to Ninjas

The ninja made their reputation during the Japanese civil wars. They worked for anybody—often for both sides at the same time. In addition to being scouts, a favorite ninja job was to sneak into a castle under siege and cause as much chaos as possible. Dressed like the enemy, they made their way into enemy camps to set fires, start rebellions in the ranks, steal flags, and generally keep the pressure on their opponents so that when the army outside stormed the gates, the defenders would give up without a fight.

Ninjas used weapons that were uniquely suited to them. They wore claws on their gloves to help them fight and climb. Because the ownership of weapons was forbidden to all but the samurai, ninjas used a common farming tool called a sickle for much of their fighting. And, of course, they used the throwing stars that everybody sees in the movies, though the real ninjas weren't nearly as accurate as their Hollywood counterparts. They also used invisibility weapons, usually an eggshell filled with an eye irritant or a bit of gunpowder with a fuse in case they had to make a quick getaway.

Eventually the Japanese civil wars came to an end, and the ninjas found themselves out of a job. The ninjas were gone but certainly not forgotten. The exploits of the ninja made their way into popular literature and eventually into legend.

Ninja Fact and Fiction

The ninja were feared for their ability to assassinate their rivals, but there was never a documented case of any ruler being killed by a ninja. They tried, of course, but they were never successful.

Although ninjas are typically thought to be male, there were female ninjas as well. Whether male or female, one thing is certain: Ninjas didn't run around in black pajamas as Hollywood would have you believe.

This misconception originated in Kabuki Theater. During shows, the prop movers wore all black to shift things around while the play was going on. Everybody was supposed to ignore the people in black, pretending they were invisible. So when it became time for ninjas to be played in the theater, they wore the same black dress as the prop movers to symbolize their gift of invisibility. The crowds bought it, and the black ninja suit was born.

The exploits of the ninja came to the West mainly after World War II. Like the Japanese theater, Hollywood's version of the ninja portrayed them either as an almost unbeatable mystical foe or as a clumsy fighter that the hero of the movie could take on singlehandedly.

Although there are martial arts schools that teach ninja techniques, the ninja have faded into history and legend.

Three Pirate Myths You Can Blame on R. L. Stevenson

If Robert Louis Stevenson is unlucky enough to be sharing the afterlife with pirates, he's likely answering some uncomfortable questions. His novel *Treasure Island* gave us a host of pirate myths that would make real pirates shiver their timbers.

1. Pirates had parrots perched on their shoulders. The idea that pirates and parrots go together is not entirely unfounded. Like other seafarers of the time, pirates were awestruck by colorful birds in tropical ports. Parrots made good souvenirs, bribes, or gifts, and they fetched a nice price back in Europe. But other than Long John Silver, pirates didn't stomp around with parrots secured to their shoulders. A large, squawking bird would have made firing a cannon or running the rigging difficult, to say the least.

2. Pirates ran around yelling, "Fifteen men on the dead man's chest. Yo-ho-ho and a bottle of rum." Most every sailor sang sea shanties, which provided both a diversion and a rhythm for hoisting anchors and hauling bowlines. But fictional pirates and pirate wannabes have been singing this particular song only since Stevenson made up a few lines for *Treasure Island*. A writer named Young E. Allison later expanded the snippet into a six-stanza poem titled "The Derelict." In 1901, the tune was added when the poem was used in a musical version of *Treasure Island*.

3. Pirates marked treasure maps with an "X." To pass the time in the rainy Scottish Highlands, Stevenson drew a treasure map and then made up stories (which he later wrote down) for his stepson. But it is unlikely that real pirates ever drew maps to locate their buried treasure. Not a single pirate treasure map has ever been found, and pirates would not likely have risked alerting others to their booty. Scholars doubt that pirates buried much treasure in the first place. Although they returned from raids flush with loot, they blew through it quickly because they didn't expect to live long enough to spend it in retirement.

A Not-So-Down-Under Invention

Contrary to popular myth, lore, and Australian drinking songs, boomerangs, or "The Throwing Wood," as proponents prefer to call them, did not originate down under.

The colonists, adventurers, prisoners, and explorers who ventured into the heart of the Australian wilderness may be excused for believing that the local aborigines created these little aerodynamic marvels, considering the proficiency with which they used the wooden devices to bring down wild game and wilder colonials. The gyroscopic precision with which boomerangs were (and still are) crafted by primitive peoples continues to intrigue and astonish those who come in contact with the lightweight, spinning missiles, which—if thrown correctly—actually will return to their throwers.

Many Returns

As a weapon of war and especially as a tool for hunting small game, the boomerang has been around for nearly

10,000 years. In fact, evidence of boomerangs has been discovered in almost every nook and cranny in the world. Pictures of boomerangs can be found in Neolithic-era cave drawings in France, Spain, and Poland. The *lagobolon* ("hare club") was commonly used by nobles in Crete around 2000 BC. And King Tut, ruler of Egypt around 1350 BC, had a large collection of boomerangs—several of which were found when his tomb was discovered in the 1920s.

The Greek mythological hero Hercules is depicted tossing about a curved *clava* ("throwing stick") on pottery made during the Homeric era. Carthaginian invaders in the 2nd century BC were bombarded by Gallic warriors who rained *catela* ("throwing clubs"). The Roman historian Horace describes a flexible wooden device used by German tribes, saying "if thrown by a master, it returns to the one who threw it." Roman Emperor Caesar Augustus's favorite author, Virgil, also describes a similar curved missile weapon in use by natives of the province of Hispania.

However, Europeans can no more claim the invention of the boomerang than their Australian cousins can. Archaeologists have unearthed evidence of boomerang use throughout Neolithic-era Africa, from Sudan to Niger, and from Cameroon to Morocco. And tribes in southern India, the American southwest, Mexico, and Java all used the boomerang, or something very similar, and for the same purposes.

Australians, however, can be credited with bringing the boomerang to the attention of the modern world. They helped popularize it both as a child's toy and as an item for sport. A World Cup is held every other year, and enthusiasts and scientists still compete to design, construct, and throw the perfect boomerang.

Though the weapon or toy known today as the boomerang did not originate in Australia—or at least did not originate exclusively there—the word itself is Australian. Boomerang is a blending of the words, *woomerang* and *bumarin*, terms used by different groups of Australian aborigines for their little wooden wonders.

The Origins of the Game

It was long believed that Mr. Abner Doubleday invented baseball in 1839. While we now know this is not true, we still don't know exactly how baseball came about.

Games involving sticks and balls go back thousands of years. They've been traced to the Mayans in the Americas and to Egypt at the time of the Pharaohs. There are historical references to Greeks, Chinese, and Vikings "playing ball." And a woodcut from 14th-century France shows what seem to be a batter, pitcher, and fielders.

Starting with Stoolball

By the 18th century, references to "baseball" began to appear in British publications. In an 1801 book entitled *The Sports and Pastimes of the People of England*, Joseph Strutt claimed that baseball-like games could be traced back to the 14th century, and that the then-current form of baseball was a descendant of a British game called "stoolball." The earliest known reference to stoolball is in a 1330 poem by William Pagula, who recommended to priests that the game be forbidden within churchyards.

In stoolball (which is still played in England, mostly by women), a batter stands before a target, perhaps an upturned stool, while another player pitches a ball to the batter. If the batter hits the ball (with a bat or his/her hand) and it is caught by a fielder, the batter is out. Ditto if the pitched ball hits a stool leg.

The Game Evolves

It seems that stoolball eventually split into two different styles. One became English "base-ball," which turned into "rounders" in England but evolved into "town ball" when it reached the United States. The other side of stoolball turned into cricket.

From town ball came the two styles that dominated base-ball's development: the Massachusetts Game and the New York Game. The former had no foul or fair territory; runners were put out by being hit with a thrown ball when off the base ("soaking"), and as soon as one out was made, the offense and defense switched sides. The latter established the concept of foul lines, and each team was given three "outs" to an inning. Perhaps more significantly, soaking was eliminated in favor of the more gentlemanly tag. The two versions coexisted in the first three decades of the 19th century, but when the Manhattanites codified their rules in 1845, it became easier for more and more groups to play the New York style.

A book printed in France in 1810 laid out the rules for a bat/base/running game called "poison ball," in which there were two teams of eight to ten players, four bases (one called "home"), a pitcher, a batter, and flyball outs. Different variations of the game went by different names: "Tip-cat" and "trap ball" were notable for how important the bat had become. It was no longer used merely to avoid hurting one's hand; it had become a real cudgel, to swat the ball a long way.

The Knickerbocker Club

In the early 1840s, Alexander Cartwright, a New York City engineer, was one of a group who met regularly to play baseball, and he may have been the mastermind behind organizing, formalizing, and writing down the rules of the game. The group called themselves The Knickerbocker Club, and their constitution, enacted on September 23, 1845, led the way for the game we know today.

The Myth Begins

Even though the origins of baseball are murky, there's one thing we know for sure: Abner Doubleday had nothing to do with it. The Mills Commission was organized in 1905 by Albert Spalding to search for a definitive American source for baseball. They "found" it in an ambiguous letter spun by a Cooperstown resident (who turned out to be crazy). But Doubleday wasn't even in Cooperstown when the author of the letter said he had invented the game. Also, "The Boy's Own Book" presented the rules for a baseball-like game ten years before Doubleday's alleged "invention." Chances are, we'll never know for sure how baseball came to be the game it is today.

"Rum, Sodomy, and the Lash"

Is it possible that Prime Minister Winston Churchill, whose favorite port in a storm was any one with abundant alcohol, would dish out a disparaging dictum about the British Royal Navy?

When Great Britain was a dominant naval power, it was said that Britannia ruled the waves with a navy rich in resources and bathed in tradition. Therefore, it came as a shock to the

British population when it was widely reported that Winston Churchill was of the opinion that the only true traditions that the Royal Navy observed were "rum, sodomy, and the lash."

In fact, Churchill's dissenters perpetrated the origin of this myth-quote. In the 1940s, while he was serving as prime minister and his country was fighting for its very survival, Churchill's political foes concocted an amusing smear campaign that focused on his apparent disdain for and distrust of the navy. According to Churchill's competitors, young Winston had been denied entry to the Royal Naval College because he suffered from a speech impediment, and the scars from that snub never healed.

That wound still riled him when he allegedly rose in the House of Commons and delivered a scathing speech that ridiculed the Royal Navy and its traditions, which he summarized as the equivalent of alcohol, sex, and torture. But the entire incident proved to be fabricated. Records show that Churchill never attempted to join the navy, and documents concur that he never used the House of Commons as a platform to voice his opinions on the Admiralty. Yet, the line remains one of the most popular quotes attributed to Churchill. Its fame was cemented when he supposedly confided to his assistant, Anthony Montague-Browne, that although he had never spoken those words, he certainly wished he had.

Benedict Arnold's Last Fictional Words

Here's the story: On his deathbed in 1801, Benedict Arnold donned his old Continental Army togs and repented his treason with the words "Let me die in this old uniform in which I fought my battles. May God forgive me for ever having put on another." And here's the truth.

While serving as a general in the Continental Army during the American Revolution, Benedict Arnold switched sides when he attempted to surrender the American fort at West Point to the British. Twenty years later, as Arnold lay dying of dropsy at home in England, his wife, Margaret, could do little to relieve his terminal suffering and delirium. When she broke the sad news to his sons in America, she described him as barely able to breathe, suffering from "a very dreadful nervous symptom." The same letter says nothing about a uniform or a dying wish.

Another weakness in the story: It sounds exactly like what later generations of patriotic Americans would like to hear. It also sounds far too noble for Arnold, who had turned his coat seeking opportunity and ended up finding little.

If people want a feel-good story about Arnold, they should note that this brave, energetic officer did the colonial cause far more good than harm. By the time he betrayed the colonies, much had gone wrong for the British (thanks in part to Benedict himself). Arnold was in heavy debt and felt slighted in favor of mediocre officers. Most good officers rise above such frustrations, but the temperamental Arnold chose high treason instead.

His unsavory reputation had followed him from Canada to England, making him a tolerated but unpopular figure. None of his postwar businesses had thrived, and with Napoleon running amok, Arnold's death and burial were relatively insignificant.

As a Wise Man Once Said . . .

If you ever hear someone say, "Mark Twain once said . . . ," chances are that what follows was never said by Twain.

Mark Twain is a *quote magnet*, a person to whom quotations are often falsely ascribed. And the process of ascribing quotations to such people is sometimes called *Churchillian drift*, a term coined by quotation maven Nigel Rees in reference to Winston Churchill, another powerful quote magnet. Others who attract credit for a lot of quotes include Benjamin Franklin, Yogi Berra, Abraham Lincoln, Oscar Wilde, Satchel Paige, and George Bernard Shaw.

Examples of quotations falsely attributed to quote magnets include:

🦆 "The coldest winter I ever spent was a summer in San Francisco." Falsely attributed to Mark Twain. No one knows who first changed Twain's similar, but less eloquent, comment about Paris into this pithy form.

🦆 "Donny Osmond has Van Gogh's ear for music." Falsely attributed to Orson Welles, but actually said by Billy Wilder in 1964 about actor Cliff Osmond (no relation): "Cliff has the musical ear of Van Gogh."

🦆 "If you're not a liberal when you're 25, you have no heart. If you're not a conservative by the time you're 35, you have no brain." Falsely attributed to Winston Churchill; probably a paraphrase of a quote by historian and statesman François Guizot.

Why are such people quote magnets? Well, often a quote can be "improved" by attributing it to a famous person. A pithy bit of wisdom sounds better if it comes from Abraham Lincoln rather than your Uncle Joe. Even a quote from a famed director like Billy Wilder can be improved by attributing it to an even more famous director (and changing the subject to a more famous Osmond).

The problem has only worsened in the digital age, where myths and false attributions multiply online like viruses until it's almost impossible to find the truth. The lesson is to never trust a quotation unless the date and circumstances of its utterance are given. Perhaps the subject of quote magnets is best summed up by George Bernard Shaw: "I tell you I have been misquoted everywhere, and the inaccuracies are chasing me around the world."

The Bard said many profound things, like "that's one small step for a man, one giant leap for mankind," and "either you like bacon or you're wrong."

"A witty quote proves nothing."
—Voltaire

Easy History Quiz

This is just a warm-up quiz. Our later quizzes will separate the trivia buffs from the trivia bimbos.

1. The year 1095 is significant because in that year the Magna Carta was signed.

       True   False

2. The stock market crash preceding the Great Depression happened on October 29, 1929.

       True   False

3. The "D" in D-day stands for "Destruction."

       True   False

4. King Charlemagne was a Frenchman.

       True   False

5. In 1863, the Emancipation Proclamation declared all slaves in the United States to be free.

       True   False

6. William of Normandy invaded England in 1066.

       True   False

7. The War of 1812 began in 1812.

       True   False

8. The last Chinese emperor was forced to abdicate in 1949.

       True   False

9. Julius Caesar was assassinated in 44 BC.

       True   False

10. The year 1215 is significant because in that year the Magna Carta was signed.

       True   False

Answers

1. False. Pope Urban II initiated the First Crusade in 1095.

2. True. In a single day's trading, billions of dollars were wiped out.

3. False. The letter is simply derived from the word it precedes. The same is true for H-hour.

4. False. Charlemagne was Frankish, not French. France did not yet exist in his time.

5. False. It didn't free them all. It was the Thirteenth Amendment, passed in 1864, that abolished slavery.

6. True. William's army won a decisive victory at the Battle of Hastings in that year. He was crowned on Christmas Day, 1066.

7. True. Of course it did. That's why it's called the War of 1812.

8. False. His *1912* abdication ended the 2,000-year-old imperial system.

9. True. He was stabbed 23 times.

10. True. In that year, King John agreed to the Great Charter—placing him and all future English sovereigns within the rule of law.

CHAPTER 4

Survival of the Stupidest

You can be dumb. You can be smart. You can be smart and have dumb ideas and you can be dumb and have smart ideas. You can have dumb ideas about being smart or even dumb ideas about being dumb. That's all fine. But as life has taught you by now, *the dumb will always outnumber the smart*. This is your first rule of survival.

Another fine rule: don't expect Dumb to smarten up. That's like waiting for a monkey to start hammering out Shakespeare on a typewriter spontaneously—the odds aren't in your favor.* Dumb is pervasive, like dandelions. It gets in your laundry and moves in next door. You will never, ever escape Dumb, and it will probably eventually kill you. Want some examples of death by being Dumb?

* The infinite monkey theorem states that, given an infinite length of time, a monkey hitting keys on a typewriter will eventually compose the entire works of William Shakespeare.

Death by Bottle Cap According to friends and family, Tennessee Williams, the award-winning author of *The Glass Menagerie*, *A Streetcar Named Desire*, and *Cat on a Hot Tin Roof*, had a habit of opening the cap of his eye-drop bottles with his teeth, then tilting his head backward to moisten his eyes. The system worked until February 25, 1983, when Williams accidentally inhaled the cap and choked to death.

Death by Lightbulb On March 11, 1978, Claude Francois, a popular French pop singer, was standing in a filled bathtub in his Paris apartment when he noticed a broken lightbulb. Obsessed with orderliness, Francois immediately tried to change the bulb, electrocuting himself in the process.

Death by Frozen Chicken A true renaissance man, Francis Bacon was a respected statesman, scientist, philosopher, and author whose works include *Novum Organum* and *The New Atlantis*. In March 1626, Bacon came up with the bright idea that meat could be preserved by freezing it. To test his theory, he went to town, bought a gutted chicken, then stood in inclement weather and stuffed the bird with snow. He promptly developed pneumonia and died a few months later.

Death by Martini In 1941, during a party aboard an ocean liner bound for Brazil, author Sherwood Anderson accidentally swallowed a martini olive, toothpick and all. The tiny sliver of wood embedded in Anderson's intestines, leading to peritonitis, which ultimately killed him.

Death by Scarf A groundbreaking and influential dancer in her day, Isadora Duncan was strangled by her own scarf on September 14, 1927, when the excessively long and flowing garment became tangled in the rear wheel of the car in which she was riding.

Death by Full Bladder Tycho Brahe, a Danish nobleman and influential astronomer, suffered from recurring bladder problems. In 1601, he attended a formal banquet and was unable to visit the bathroom to relieve himself before the festivities started. Supposedly, he drank heavily over the course of the evening and managed to hold his urine for the duration. This proved to be a fatal mistake—the strain on his bladder resulted in a serious infection, which killed him 11 days later. A more scientific theory, formulated after his body was exhumed in 1996, suggests death by mercury poisoning.

Death by Embrace Considered one of the greatest poets China has ever known, Li Bai was also a raging drunk. Legend holds that one evening in the year 762, while cruising down the Yangtze River, the inebriated writer fell off his boat and drowned when he tried to embrace the moon's reflection on the water. It's a great story, but recent evidence indicates it's more likely that he died from complications of old age.

Death by Overcoat A tailor by trade, Franz Reichelt developed a garment that was both an overcoat and a parachute. On February 4, 1912, he decided to test his invention by jumping off the Eiffel Tower. He told the authorities that he was going to use a mannequin first, but decided at the last minute to try it himself. Confident that his invention would work, Reichelt calmly stepped off a platform and plunged to his death.

What's the Matter with Brain Matter?

Contrary to popular belief, adults can and do grow new brain cells. Oddly enough, some of the first people to recognize that brains are not set in stone were crooked canary sellers. Because male canaries sing and female canaries usually do not, only the male canaries fetch a handsome price at pet stores. During the 1940s and '50s, some enterprising bird importers tried injecting female canaries with testosterone in hopes of giving them the gift of song. The scam actually worked: The masculinized female canaries sang just long enough to be sold as males to hoodwinked pet-store owners and their unsuspecting customers.

In the mid-1970s, when scientists at Rockefeller University repeated the canary sellers' testosterone "experiments," they discovered that the region of the brain responsible for singing was much larger in male canaries than in females. The injected female birds generated glial cells (which give structural support to the brain) and new neurons in that region. Subsequent research at Cornell University confirmed that this was not just stuff for the birds: All vertebrate brains, whether canary or human, house precursor cells, which can be stimulated to develop into new neurons, just as they would during embryonic development. Adult neurogenesis holds the tantalizing promise of rebuilding brain cells destroyed by injury, stroke, or degenerative diseases such as Alzheimer's or Parkinson's—a goal long considered to be the Holy Grail of medical research.

A Bigger Brain Doesn't Translate to a Smarter Person

If you're someone who has an oversized noggin—and displays it like a trophy—we really hate to rain on your parade: You are not smarter than the rest of us. Scientific studies continue to show that size isn't everything where the human brain is concerned.

History Lessons

Sure, it might be easy to assume that a colossal cranium is capable of holding more intelligence—just by sheer mass. History suggests otherwise. William H. Calvin, a theoretical neurophysiologist and affiliate professor emeritus at the University of Washington School of Medicine, points to notable periods in the historical timeline when the brain mass of ancient humans greatly increased, but toolmaking smarts did not. Although *Homo sapiens* in Africa 200,000 years ago had developed a brain size comparable to that of contemporary people, they continued to use the same crude, round-edged rocks for some 150,000 years before graduating to points, needles, harpoons, and hooks. You can't exactly say those bigger-brained primates were the sharpest tools in the shed.

Modern Science Weighs In

As for modern people, advancements in magnetic resonance imaging (MRI)-based brain scans are giving researchers more pertinent data about the relationship between brain size and intelligence. (Before MRI, researchers had to measure the outside of a person's head to estimate brain size, or wait until that person died to get an accurate measurement.) A 2004 study conducted by researchers at the University of California-Irvine and the University of New Mexico was one of the first to use MRI technology to demonstrate that it's not overall brain size that counts, but brain organization.

How so? The researchers used MRI to get structural scans of the study participants' brains, and then compared those scans to respective scores on standard IQ tests. What they discovered was that human intelligence is less about total girth and more about the volume and specific location of gray-matter tissue across the brain. It appears there are several "smart" areas of the brain related to IQ, and having more gray matter in those locations is one of the things that makes us, well, smarter.

Undoubtedly, the relationship between brain size and intelligence will continue to be studied and debated, but some in the medical field now believe that brain size is purely a function of genetics and doesn't result in a greater intellect. Researchers at Harvard Medical School have even been able to identify two of the genes (beta-catenin and ASPM) that regulate brain size.

So if you've got a big head, don't be so quick to get a big head. It turns out that Albert Einstein's brain weighed only 2.7 pounds. That's 10 percent smaller than average.

The Intelligence on IQ Tests

IQ scores are best known as quantitative representations of a person's intelligence. Yet the original IQ test was intended to predict future scholastic achievement, not intelligence.

The famed dumbbell Forrest Gump had an IQ of 75, but he did pretty well for himself. He was a military hero, savvy businessman, exceptional table tennis player, and beloved son, husband, and father. An IQ test is supposed to measure intelligence, but there is much debate over what an IQ score actually means.

A person's intelligence quotient is calculated according to his or her performance on a standardized test. This means that the score is not derived from how many questions are answered correctly but on how many the person gets right relative to others who have taken the same test. IQ tests are usually standardized so that 100 is the mean score, and half of the scores lie within 10 points of the mean—so half the population has an IQ between 90 and 110. "IQ test" actually refers to a number of popular tests that are standardized in a similar fashion, such as the Wechsler or Stanford-Binet tests. The first IQ test was developed in the late 1800s, hand-in-hand with the appearance of special-education programs in schools. Administrators needed a reliable way to identify those who were unable to learn as easily or quickly as others. From the beginning, then, IQ tests were meant to measure one's ability to perform academic tasks; this is not necessarily synonymous with intelligence.

Kinds of Smart

IQ test questions measure such functions as short-term memory, vocabulary, perceptual speed, and visual-spatial reasoning. These are all skills that help a person succeed in a school, work, or even social environment. Not surprisingly, high IQ scores are positively correlated with one's future academic success. They are also correlated, though not as strongly, with the socioeconomic status of one's parents, as well as on future income and future job performance.

Many researchers have pointed out that IQ tests neglect to calculate many types of talent that could also fall under the "intelligence" heading. Psychologist Howard Gardner

developed his theory of multiple intelligences, which include linguistic, logical-mathematical, spatial, bodily-kinesthetic, musical, interpersonal, intrapersonal, and naturalist. Many multiple-intelligence tests try to include indicators of "books smarts," "street smarts," and "creativity smarts."

Relax. At least you have good spatial intelligence.

Testing IQ Tests

The reliability of IQ tests as meters of intelligence is also suspect because, on average, African American, Native

American, and other minority or immigrant populations score lower than populations of Euro-American descent. These minority groups tend to come from areas where there is a high dropout rate and limited access to quality education. IQ tests are administered in standard English, which partly accounts for the low scores (especially in the verbal section) among people who speak other dialects of English or English as a second language.

The Dumb Blonde Stereotype

How did a woman with blonde hair become synonymous with "airhead"? If you were to do an informal survey of Caucasian American women, you would find that one out of three has some shade of blonde hair. Of these, only a small percentage are natural blondes. The rest lighten their locks with the help of chemicals, partaking in a ritual that goes back thousands of years. It turns out that in ancient Greece, blonde hair was all the rage.

Dyeing to Be Blonde

The original blonde bombshell was Aphrodite, the Greek goddess of love. Aphrodite embodied the erotic. She was said to have risen out of the ocean in a wave of sea foam (which explains her white skin and flowing blonde tresses). Aphrodite's paleness set her apart from her otherwise dark-haired Mediterranean worshippers. What better way to revere than to imitate? Hellenic women (and men) used saffron, oils, lye, and even mud to yellow their hair. The demand for blonde hair was so great that the Romans kidnapped fair-haired barbarians just to keep their wig-makers well-supplied. Thus began one of the longest lasting fashion trends in Western culture.

Since then, the only time that blonde has gone out of style was during the Middle Ages. It was considered sinful for a woman to show her hair in public, much less treat it with bleaches. The Catholic Church tried to make blondness a symbol of chastity and innocence. The Virgin Mary was depicted with golden hair (as was Jesus at times). However, despite sermons and writings denouncing the evil, carnal power of colored hair, it did not lose its allure. By the time of Queen Elizabeth I, the use of hair dyes was in vogue again.

Playing the Part

In the 1700s, a Parisian courtesan by the name of Rosalie Duthe became the first famously dumb blonde. It is said that she never spoke but could seduce any man simply by looking at him and entrancing him with her elaborately styled golden hair. She was parodied in intellectual circles and was even featured in a comic play where she became the laughingstock of Paris. As women of "ill repute" increasingly colored their hair to boost business, the association between colored hair and cheap, wanton behavior deepened.

Hooray for Hollywood!

It took Hollywood to combine innocence and sexuality. Starlets like Jean Harlow and Marlene Dietrich paved the way for our own modern-day goddess—and ultimate blonde icon—Marilyn Monroe. Even today, decades after her death, she remains as alluring and enduring as Aphrodite herself. A succession of Tinseltown deities—including Brigitte Bardot, Farrah Fawcett, and Paris Hilton—all fit the "dumb blonde" stereotype placed on Monroe. There is, of course, no connection between a woman's hair color and her intelligence. Marilyn Monroe was, in fact, a woman of calculating intelligence. (For instance, she was known to relax between shoots by reading weighty authors such as Thomas Paine and Heinrich Heine.)

There is, however, a kernel of truth to the "dumb blonde" stereotype. A group of French academics conducted a study that proves blonde hair does influence intelligence—men's intelligence. It turns out that the sight of a blonde woman makes men dumber! Men were shown a series of photographs of women with various hair colors and then given a series of basic knowledge tests. Those who were shown blonde women scored the lowest. In the end, the joke seems to be on men.

"Never attribute to malice that which is adequately explained by stupidity."

—Hanlon's razor

"We are all born ignorant, but one must work hard to remain stupid."

—Benjamin Franklin

"Brains are an asset, if you hide them."

—Mae West

"Somebody else's ignorance is bliss."

—Jack Vance

"A computer once beat me at chess, but it was no match for me at kickboxing."

—Emo Philips

"Anything too stupid to be said is sung."

—Voltaire

"The trouble ain't that there is too many fools, but that the lightning ain't distributed right."

—Mark Twain

A Matter of Perspective

An obviously drunk man was driving a van that had already sustained considerable damage. The Georgia police officer that stopped the van discovered several outstanding

warrants on the driver. When the drunkard was brought in to the police station, he told the cops he didn't even have change for a phone call. Incredibly, the man had won $3 million in a lottery five months ago.

As the man told it, he had so far received an initial payment of $94,000. First he dropped $30,000 in the Atlantic City casinos. Next he spent another $30,000 on the van, which he later rolled because he had drunk copious amounts of expensive French wine approximately $10,000 worth). Curious, the cop asked what had happened to the other $24,000. "Oh," the guy replied. "I spent the other $24,000 foolishly."

Idiot-Proof (or Not)

In some ways, the word *idiot* has remained remarkably consistent. The earliest meaning in the *Oxford English Dictionary*—"a person without learning; an ignorant, uneducated man; a simple man; a clown"—is not far from its contemporary sense as "a term of reprobation for one who speaks or acts in what the speaker considers an irrational way, or with extreme stupidity or folly; a blockhead, an utter fool." A new idiot would not surprise observers of old idiots, and vice versa.

The word has its origins in the Greek *idiotes*, meaning "commoner" or "layman" and, hence, one who is ignorant or ill-informed. It came to English from the French *idiot* by way of the Latin *idiota*, which, similar to the Greek, means "an uneducated, ignorant person."

While staying on the same general thoroughfare, the term has gone down some interesting alleyways over the years. In some cases, it has named a profession, similar to a clown, fool, or jester (this sense inspired the term *idiot's hood*, a predecessor of *dunce cap*. There have been variations such as *idiot boy*, *idiot fool*, and *idiot man*. Other *idiot* uses include: *idiot asylum* (an unkind term for a mental asylum), *idiot box* (a TV set), *idiotize* (to become, let us say, closer in intelligence to a brick), and *idiot stick* (a shovel).

Although *idiot* is now more or less interchangeable with any of the innumerable dummy-denoting descriptors, it was once a quasi-technical medical term. In the not-so-distant past, the word functioned as part of an IQ-based intelligence classification system. Up until the early 1970s, psychologists used the terms *moron*, *imbecile*, and *idiot* to distinguish between different levels of intellectual disability. This system was eventually recognized as insensitive, and the terms were replaced by less pejorative labels.

In addition to its psychological use, *idiot* boasts some high-profile appearances in classic literature, as well as pop culture. Originally written in Russian, the title of Fyodor Dostoyevsky's 1868 novel is translated as *The Idiot* in English. It is said that *The Idiot*'s idiot, Prince Myshkin, represents Dostoyevsky's desire to depict "a positively good man"—not quite the sort of idiot we're used to. The title of

Iggy Pop and David Bowie's album *The Idiot* is supposedly inspired by the novel. More recent plugs for *idiot* come from rock band Green Day's album *American Idiot*, as well as the Broadway play it inspired. An amusing variation of the word is *Idiocracy*, coined as the title of a 2006 Mike Judge movie that gave a vision of a future America that makes our current population seem like a collection of Einsteins.

Brainless Bad Guys

This collection of crime-related gaffes puts the "dumb" in dumbfound.

Digitized Dummy

They say a picture is worth a thousand words. Sometimes it's worth even more. In 2003, when a Walmart in Long Island, New York, discovered that $2,000 worth of digital cameras had been lifted from their store, they went straight to the videotape. There they found images of a male and female suspect but couldn't identify either due to the tape's grainy nature. Then they spotted something of interest: At one point during the heist, the female accomplice had taken pictures with a demonstration camera. Her subject? Her partner in crime, of course. When the digital information was fed into a printer, out popped a high-quality color image of a balding man with a mustache. The 36-year-old crook was subsequently identified through a tip line and charged with grand larceny. Like Narcissus, the love of his own image brought him down.

Leave Only Footsteps

Sometimes, ambition can impede the job at hand. According to prosecutors, in 2005, a 23-year-old man filled out a job application while waiting for a pie at a Las Vegas pizza parlor. Then, out of nowhere, the man flashed a gun and demanded that the cashier give him all the money inside her cash drawer. He fled the scene $200 richer. A witness recorded his license plate, and the robber was arrested at home shortly thereafter. But this lucky break wasn't really necessary because he'd jotted down his real name and address on the job application.

Statute of Style Limitations

A security guard working at Neiman Marcus in White Plains, New York, apprehended a young woman in 2007 for shoplifting. He caught up with the 19-year-old outside of the store and accused her of stealing a pair of $250 jeans. While he waited for police to arrive, the accused railed bitterly against the guard. According to the police report, she was convinced that she was immune from prosecution based on a legal technicality, stating triumphantly, "It's too late. I already left the store!"

Big-Time Loser

Some criminals don't know when to stop. In 2007, a New York man was pulled over for a traffic stop and racked up a bunch of criminal infractions in the process. He was intoxicated; not wearing a seat belt; driving toward oncoming traffic lanes with an open beer container by his side; driving with an expired inspection sticker and with license plates from another car; operating an uninsured vehicle; and transporting his two-year-old daughter without benefit of a car seat or a fastened seat belt.

Indiscriminate Crook

In 2007, an ex-con pulled a fake handgun on two victims and demanded their cash. The only problem was, they were two uniformed New York City police officers. The officers responded by drawing their real weapons, and the mugger surrendered after a brief, but tense, standoff.

Crime Doesn't Pay

In 2007, a thief entered a Fairfield, Connecticut, Dunkin' Donuts. Intent on snaring the contents of its cash register, the would-be crook handed the clerk a note stating that he was carrying a gun and a bomb, and he would use both if he didn't receive cash. With that, the heist meister grabbed the entire machine from the counter and made his getaway. But there was one significant problem: The clueless criminal had made off with an adding machine instead of the cash register.

CHAPTER 5

Who Would Eat That Garbage?

You would, apparently. Haven't you ever found it strange—the things we keep in our cupboards, put on our plates, and cram in our mouths? We feign disgust at the oddities on foreign menus, but think about what a slice of cheese is: a congealed mass of stinky, spoiled milk. What's honey? Twice-regurgitated insect vomit. How about the egg—that slimy, reproductive cul de sac?

And have you ever looked down at your delicious, refreshing, lime Jell-O dessert and connected it with the most worthless leftover parts found on the slaughterhouse floor? Now you will.

Think about it.

Is Jell-O Really Made from Horses?

Could this fun, wiggly dessert be the final resting place for the likes of Black Beauty and Mister Ed? Sure. But let's not be too picky—any creature with bones can become Jell-O. It's an equal opportunity dessert.

Jell-O is made from gelatin, which is processed collagen. Collagen makes your bones strong and your skin elastic and stretchy (there's that jiggly wiggle). To make gelatin, you take bones, skin, tendons, and whatnot from animals (primarily cows or pigs), grind everything up, wash and soak it in acid (and also lime, if cow parts are used), and throw it in a vat to boil. The acid or lime breaks down the components of the ground animal pieces, and the result is gelatin, among other things. The gelatin conveniently rises to the top of this mixture of acid and animal parts, creating an easy-to-remove film.

In the Victorian era, when gelatin was really catching on, it was sold in the film state. People had to clarify the gelatin by boiling it with egg whites and eggshells, which took a lot of time. In 1845, a crafty inventor patented a powdered gelatin, which was to be extracted from the bones of geese. In 1897, this powdered gelatin was named Jell-O and went on to become the line of dessert products that, to this day, we always have room for. Why does the list of ingredients in Jell-O include gelatin and not cow and pig pieces? Because the U.S. federal government does not consider gelatin an animal product, since it is extensively processed. Gelatin is also found in gummy bears candy, cream cheese, marshmallows, and other foods.

What if you like Jell-O, cream cheese, marshmallows, and such, but would rather not eat the boiled bones and skin of animals? There are alternatives. Agar and carrageenan are made from seaweed and can be used to create delicious gelatin-like goodies. So while it's unlikely your Jell-O contains traces of Mister Ed or Black Beauty, it could test positive for Wilbur or Elsie.

Thanks, I'll Just Have Crackers

Granted, to some people a Twinkie probably looks pretty disgusting. But at least Twinkies don't slither around or smell like poo. Here's a sampling of some of the weirdest foods in the world.

Nutria

The nutria is a semi-aquatic rodent about the size of a cat with bright orange teeth. After World War II, they were sold in the United States as "Hoover Hogs." Since the animals chew up crops and cause erosion, in 2002 Louisiana officials offered $4 for every nutria killed. Still, their meat is rumored to be lean and tasty.

Uok

The coconut: Without it, the piña colada and macaroons wouldn't exist. Neither would the Uok, a golf ball-size, coconut-dwelling, bitter-tasting worm enjoyed by some Filipinos. Just pull one down from a mangrove tree, salt, and sauté!

Balut

If you're craving a midnight snack, skip the cheesecake and enjoy a boiled duck embryo. Folks in Cambodia will let eggs develop until the bird inside is close to hatching, and then they boil it and enjoy the egg with a cold beer.

One Smooth Frog

In Bolivia and Peru, Lake Titicaca frogs are harvested for a beverage affectionately referred to as "Peruvian Viagra." The frogs are plopped in a blender with some spices and the resulting brown goo is served up in a tall glass. Turn on the Barry White . . .

Duck Blood Soup

Bright red goose blood is the main ingredient in this Vietnamese soup. A few veggies and spices round out the frothy meal.

The Man Who Ate an Airplane

Michel Lotito was a French entertainer better known as "Monsieur Mangetout"—which translates to "Mr. Eats All." As you can guess, Lotito got the nickname because of his habit of eating just about anything—beds, television sets, bicycles, and even an entire Cessna 150 airplane. Throughout his life, it is estimated that Mr. Eats All ate around nine tons of metal.

It is said that Lotito suffered from pica, a condition that causes cravings for non-food items like dirt, chalk, and glass. In Lotito's case, it also caused cravings for metal. The disorder can be dangerous, leading to blocked intestines, lead poisoning, and other emergencies.

But doctors determined that Lotito had an extra-thick lining in his stomach and intestines, making it possible for him to eat inedible objects without as much of a risk for internal damage. He was even known to eat substances that would've been poisonous to most people.

Before he ate, Lotito would drink large amounts of mineral oil in order to help guide the foreign material through his digestive system. He would then break the objects into small pieces, and drink plenty of water while he ate.

He limited his metal intake to about one kilogram per day, so it could take a while for him to finish a "meal." It took him an entire two years to consume the Cessna, and bicycles took several sittings. Strangely, while Lotito seemed to have no trouble with metal objects, he had a hard time digesting bananas and hard-boiled eggs!

Lotito died at the age of fifty-seven. His official cause of death was "natural causes." But one must wonder if his bizarre eating habits contributed in some way.

Woman's Comfort Food Is the Foam from Couch Cushions

When Adele Edwards' parents were going through a divorce, the then ten-year-old needed a way to cope. So she turned to a rather strange source of comfort: eating foam couch cushions.

Over the last twenty-one years, the Florida mother of five has continued to eat the foam inside cushions. In one year alone, she ate through seven sofas. Edwards even stuffs pieces of foam into her purse when she leaves the house so she can snack on the substance all day.

According to her doctors, her habit is very dangerous and could even cause a fatal stomach blockage. Edwards has already had a foam blockage the size of a grapefruit that forced her to take large amounts of laxatives. When she recently also began ingesting dirt, her doctor diagnosed her with iron deficiency. Edwards now takes iron supplements and is trying therapy and hypnosis to cut down on her appetite for foam.

Deadly Delicacy

In Japan and Korea, there is a delicacy known as odori don. But to eat it, you have to be a fan of really fresh seafood. Odori don is a live squid or octopus, served on a plate while it's still moving.

To be fair, chefs remove the cephalopod's brain before it is placed on the plate, so it's not technically alive. But since it certainly was, moments earlier, still swimming, it continues to thrash around even as you pour soy sauce over it. Supposedly, this is because the creature's nerves and muscles are still active and spring to life when they come into contact with salt. But this seems to be little comfort for people who prefer their food to be inanimate.

Fans of the dish say the writhing tentacles are part of the appeal, but it should be noted that eating odori don can be dangerous. The suction cups from the octopus' tentacles can attach to the inside of your throat, choking you. In fact, the delicacy is considered so unsafe that it's banned in many countries.

Casu Marzu Maggot Cheese

Casu marzu, which means "rotting cheese" in Sardinian, is not just an aged and very smelly cheese, it is an illegal commodity in many places. Casu marzu is a runny white cheese made by injecting Pecorino Sardo cheese with cheese-eating larvae that measure about one-half inch long. Tradition calls for this cheese to be eaten with the maggots running through it. Sardinians claim these critters make the cheese creamier and that it's absolutely delicious. This cheese is widely, but not openly, eaten in Sardinia, even though the ban on it is only enforced sporadically.

Insects Are the Protein of the Future

An artisanal pasta maker in France has created a product that is flying off the shelves. The secret ingredient? Insects!

Stephanie Richard was looking for a way to create a high-protein pasta for athletes, so she decided to try adding insects to her pasta on a whim. She began creating pasta using "insect flour" by pulverizing crickets and grasshoppers and adding them to the pasta. Surprisingly, the pasta was a huge hit and Richard has had trouble keeping up with the orders.

Richard uses a mix of around seven percent insect flour and ninety-three percent spelt wheat flour, and occasionally she'll add ground mushrooms for extra flavor. The end result is a brownish pasta that tastes "like whole wheat pasta," she says.

Richard is now hoping to expand her business to keep up with the increasing demand for her pasta. "The insect is the protein of the future," she says. "It's protein of high quality that is well digested by the body." And a 2013 report by the UN Food and Agriculture Organization agrees, claiming that insects have "huge potential for feeding both people and livestock."

Is It Really Worth the Experience?

Chinju-ya restaurant in Japan is definitely a place only the most adventurous eaters would enjoy. And it may even cause a few of them to run away in horror. After all, this is a place that serves things like cooked crocodile feet, grilled piranha, and deep-fried whole salamander.

Chef Fukuoka, who has helmed the restaurant for six years, takes pride in procuring the rarest and most unusual meats from across the world. He has served everything from axolotls (a Mexican salamander) and isopods (a type of small crustacean) to black scorpions and camel meat.

For a Christmas special one year, Chef Fukuoka prepared reindeer steak and minced meat of badger served in a dry curry. Other dishes have included a whole cockroach platter, soft-boiled boar foot, whole piranhas, and bear meat stewed with chicken eggs.

And while dessert is usually a course that everyone can enjoy, at Chinju-ya you might want to skip it. For instance, the "contaminated pudding" arrives at your table infested with worms.

Amazingly, Chinju-ya is a popular restaurant among tourists and locals. And while the prices are quite high—the deep-fried salamander is $190—patrons don't seem to mind paying for the experience.

The Black Eggs of Japan

Owakudani, near Hakone, Japan, is a large volcanic caldera that formed 3,000 years ago when Mount Hakone erupted. The area is still quite geologically active, with boiling pools of water, steam vents, and fumes of sulphur dioxide and hydrogen sulphide. Yet tourists visit the inhospitable spot each year to partake in a Japanese delicacy: black boiled eggs known as kuro-tamago.

The eggs have a startling black appearance, but they're simply regular old chicken eggs. The black color comes from being boiled in the hot water pools of Owakudani.

The sulphur in the water reacts with the eggs' shells, turning them black and giving the eggs a sulphur-tinged smell and taste.

According to legend, eating the black eggs will prolong a person's life by seven years. The eggs are cooked in large batches in the waters of a spring on top of a hill, where they're loaded onto large metal crates and lowered into the spring water, which reaches temperatures of about one hundred seventy-five degrees fahrenheit, for an hour. They are then steamed at over two hundred degrees for fifteen minutes. When they're done, the shells are black, but the insides are still white and yellow like a regular boiled egg.

Visitors to the boiling site are served the eggs at a shack with small wooden tables, with a magnificent view of Mt. Fuji.

Take It Easy on the Carrots

Who knew that carrots could kill? In 1974, Basil Brown was a fitness fanatic and health food advocate in England who decided to start drinking copious amounts of carrot juice. According to reports, Brown was drinking a gallon of carrot juice a day, and also taking vitamin A supplements. According to an article in the *Ottawa Citizen*, a doctor advised him against taking the supplements because of his enlarged liver, but he ignored the advice.

After ten straight days of drinking the carrot juice, Brown died of cirrhosis of the liver. While many stories blame the overabundance of carrot juice for his death, medical experts believe the more likely cause was an overdose of vitamin A supplements.

McUrban Legends

If you are one of the more than 100 billion served at McDonald's restaurants, then you've probably heard at least one shocking (but ultimately untrue) rumor about the fast-food giant.

In the 1980s, word began circulating that McDonald's had implemented an interesting recycling program at its restaurants. Employees secretly rifled through the garbage to reclaim still-intact food-serving packages, which were then reused for subsequent orders. Those "in the know" who ate at McDonald's made sure to crumple their packages to thwart the company's nefarious money-saving scheme.

This garbage-picking anecdote is just one of the many outrageous urban legends about McDonald's. Why are the Golden Arches the subject of such scandalous stories? To start, there's the ever-present public suspicion of un-scrupulous corporations that seek to maximize profits at the expense of quality and safety. And as a high-profile multinational company perceived as spearheading the globalization movement, McDonald's is a favorite target of anti-globalization Davids looking to slay McGoliath. Here's a brief look at some of the tastier McDonald's myths that have been served up over the years.

Mmm . . . Worm Burgers

A long-standing rumor in the 1970s and '80s was that McDonald's was using ground worms as cheap filler in its hamburgers. McDonald's has always maintained that its burgers are 100 percent beef and has gone to great lengths to prove it, including procuring a letter from a U.S. Secretary of Agriculture backing the claim. Besides, McDonald's officials are quick to add, worm "meat" costs a lot more than beef, making its use in patties economically unfeasible. A similar tale was circulated in the 1990s. This time the filler ingredient was cow eyeballs, which are actually in high demand for scientific research. Consequently, their use in Big Macs would be even more cost prohibitive than worms.

What's in the shakes? It has long been alleged that Mickey D calls its milkshakes simply "shakes" because there isn't any milk or dairy products in them. The fact that they can be safely consumed by lactose-intolerant persons, say myth mongers, proves it. Among the many strange ingredients that McDonald's has purportedly substituted for milk over the years are styrofoam balls, pig fat, and the fluid from cow eyeballs (that way, nothing is wasted!). But according to McDonald's ingredient lists, its shakes do contain milk— specifically, whole milk and nonfat milk solids.

Near-Death by Bird Feathers

One of the more bizarre legends ever conjured up in the corridors of fast-food conspiracy involves an unnamed little girl in an unnamed location who had a near-death experience after eating a McFlurry (an ice-cream concoction with fruit, candy, or cookie bits whipped in). The girl, according to the story, almost died from a violent allergic reaction to bird feathers.

Doctors traced her dietary consumption leading to the reaction and pinpointed the McFlurry. It seems that they discovered through someone at McDonald's headquarters that one of the ingredients in the frozen treat is indeed bird feathers. In all versions of the tale, the girl and her whereabouts are unnamed because she doesn't exist, and the "feather" reference likely derives from the airy consistency of the product, not the mix-ins.

I'll Have a Hot Choko Pie

Another McDonald's falsity perpetrated via email is that McDonald's apple pies lack one key ingredient—apples. Rumor spreaders in the United States claim that potatoes, pears, and crackers are substituted for apples, while their Australian counterparts offer even more imaginative surrogates, such as ostrich eggs and something called chokos—a cucumber-like fruit that costs significantly more to import to Australia than the Granny Smith apples that are actually used in the handheld dessert.

From a health standpoint, there are plenty of reasons to watch what you eat at fast-food chains such as McDonald's, but an aversion to worm meat, cow eyeballs, feathers, or chokos needn't be among them.

You. It's What's for Dinner

Anthropologists debate whether cannibalism is actually a common practice in tribal cultures, or whether it happens only occasionally and under duress, as it does in so-called "civilized" society. Over the years, many people have had a taste for—and tasted—human flesh. Ready for some grisly tales? Here are ten folks who have (or are rumored to have) taken a bite.

1. Sawney Bean—Sawney Bean lived circa the 1400s in a cave near Ballantrae, in Aynshire, Scotland with his wife and their numerous children and grandchildren. According to lore, from their hideout, they robbed, killed, pickled, dried, and devoured hundreds of passersby for more than 20 years. However, some scholars argue that Bean was merely a figment of English propaganda, designed to emphasize Scottish barbarism.

2. Diego Rivera—For a period in 1904, it is said that legendary Mexican painter Diego Rivera and his friends purchased female corpses from a morgue, preferring their flavor and texture to male flesh. He believed that cannibalism would become acceptable in the future, when "man will have thrown off all of his superstitions and irrational taboos." According to one biography, he made no bones about favoring "women's brains in vinaigrette."

3. Karl Denke—"Papa Denke," as his neighbors and fellow churchgoers in Munsterberg, Germany, knew him was the organist at his local church and ran a popular boarding house. Upon his arrest in 1924, police found the remains of at least 30 former lodgers pickled in barrels in his basement. According to reports, he told police that he had eaten only human flesh for the past three years.

4. Albert Fish—Dubbed the "Gray Man" by witnesses, Albert Fish appeared to be a harmless old man, but in truth he tortured hundreds of children and reportedly killed more than a dozen throughout the East Coast. He was caught, convicted, and executed for the 1928 murder of ten-year-old Grace Budd, after he wrote to her mother and described how he killed, roasted, and ate her daughter.

5. Edward Gein—When police entered Edward Gein's Plainfield, Wisconsin, farmhouse in November 1957, they found a scene right out of a horror movie—a scene that was in fact the inspiration for the films *Psycho* and *Silence of the Lambs*. A woman's body was strung up and splayed, her heart was in a pot on the stove, and her head was in a paper bag. Human skulls were in use as bowls and decorating the bed frame, and there was a chair, lampshade, and a wastebasket made of human skin. Despite the number of corpses that must have gone into such an endeavor, Gein was only prosecuted for the murder of two local women.

6.   Joachim Kroll—This German killer lost count of how many people he had killed during his grisly career that spanned two decades, though he was sure that there had been at least 14. Kroll's activities were finally discovered in 1976 when a plumber was called to unblock the communal toilet in his apartment building, which Kroll said was clogged "with guts." The plumber pulled out a child's lungs and entrails; police found several bags full of human meat and a pot on the stove simmering with carrots, potatoes, and the hand of a four-year-old girl.

7.   Nathaniel Bar-Jonah—Born David Paul Brown in 1957 in Massachusetts, Bar-Jonah was a convicted child molester and kidnapper with a history of sadistic violence toward young boys. In 1991, he was released from the Bridgewater State Hospital and moved to Great Falls, Montana, during which time he also changed his name. After he was arrested in 1999 for lurking near an elementary school, carrying a stun gun, he became a suspect in the death of a local ten-year-old boy. A police search of his apartment yielded encrypted recipes for dishes such as "Little Boy Pot Pie." Bar-Jonah's neighbors testified that he would frequently bring them homemade casseroles or invite them to cookouts featuring funny-tasting meat he claimed to have hunted and dressed himself.

8.   Katherine Mary Knight—On February 29, 2000, an Australian woman named Katherine Mary Knight stabbed her common-law husband 37 times, skinned him, and, using the skills she learned while working in a slaughterhouse, decapitated him. She then boiled his head, roasted pieces of his corpse, and served it with vegetables to his adult children. Knight was sentenced to life in prison without parole.

9.   Armin Meiwes—In 2001, this German computer technician went online for an odd purpose. No, he didn't scan dating websites in search of a paramour; instead, he posted an advertisement for a well-built fellow who would be willing to be slaughtered and eaten. While it's hard to comprehend anyone agreeing to this, a man named Bernd-Jürgen Brandes answered the ad. Brandes willingly came to Meiwes' house, where Meiwes sliced off Brandes' penis. The pair attempted to eat it but found it inedible. After Brandes passed out from alcohol, sleeping pills, and loss of blood, Meiwes stabbed and dissected him. He ate Brandes's body over a ten-month period, garnished with potatoes and pepper sauce. Shockingly, Meiwes also filmed the event. In jail, an unrepentant Meiwes became a vegetarian.

10.   Marc Sappington—Also known in the press as the "Kansas City Vampire," Marc Sappington killed four people over his grisly career. In March 2001, what started as a run-of-the-mill armed robbery appears to have unleashed killer voices in Sappington's head. He finally succumbed to the voices in April, when he murdered a friend with a knife, and then drank his blood. Three days later, he stabbed another friend, intending to drink his blood, but lost his nerve. Later that day, he lured a 16-year-old boy to his house, shot him, hacked his body to pieces, and ate him. After his arrest, he didn't lose his appetite—in fact, Sappington asked if he could eat the investigator's leg.

There's Nothing Sweet about Them

A tip for those who rarely eat at trendy restaurants: If you see sweetbreads on the menu, don't start salivating at the thought of a warm muffin with butter dripping down the sides.

Some Thymus Gland, Anyone?

When you're thinking sweetbreads, you should picture the thymus gland or pancreas of a young sheep, cow, or pig. And once you've conjured that unappetizing image, it might be best to exhale deeply and start focusing on taking a swig or two from your glass of wine.

Sweetbreads are a delicacy enjoyed throughout the world by people with adventurous palettes, but the burger-and-fries types might not understand such culinary wanderlust. In fact, they might want to ask the question: *What in the name of the Golden Arches is a thymus gland*?

The answer isn't pretty. A thymus gland contains two lobes—one in the throat and the other near the heart. The lobe near the heart—particularly from milk-fed young calves—is considered the best to eat because of its smooth texture and mild taste; as a result, it will cost you more at that trendy restaurant. Pancreas sweetbreads, or stomach sweetbreads, are much less common than their thymus counterparts.

Sweetbreads and other edible internal organs are often grouped together using the term "offal" (which, for those still ready to vomit, isn't a word for "awful" in some foreign language). It means the "off-fall," or the off-cuts, of a carcass.

Waste Not, Want Not

Since sweetbreads aren't sweet and aren't bread, how did they get their name? This is something of a mystery. The *historie of man*, published in 1578, sheds a splash of light on the matter: "A certaine Glandulous part, called Thimus, which in Calues . . . is most pleasaunt to be eaten. I suppose we call it the sweete bread." Translation: They tasted good.

Back in those roughhewn old days—before butcher shops and grocery stores—sweetbreads weren't considered a delicacy. Families butchered their own livestock and often ate every part, including the thymus gland and pancreas. Today, sweetbreads are prepared in many ways: You can poach, roast, sear, braise, or sauté 'em, and often season them with salt, pepper, onions, garlic, or thyme.

If you want to prepare sweetbreads, we have two pieces of advice. First, sweetbreads are extremely perishable, so be sure to get them fresh and cook them within 24 hours of your purchase. Second, they're probably not the ideal dish to serve on a first date.

Have You Been Eating Stinky Socks?

It's an old mountain trick learned by generations of crafty Appalachian schoolboys: gorge yourself on ramps before going to school. By the time you get there, your breath will scare off a bear and your pores will be secreting a hellish sulphur stink so bad that chances are you'll be told to go straight back home.

Allium tricoccum (ramp, Easter onion, or wild leek, among other common names) is a wild onion that grows across a wide swath of North America. It appears in early spring and is so highly regarded in some Appalachian regions that it is the centerpiece of festivals and cook-offs. The sharply pungent vegetable is a delicious and healthy addition to any dish you might make with onions. But pungent it is. The reek of ramps is intense and long-lasting. Imagine a skunk crawled in your mouth and died. Imagine you drank a glass of dead skunk and are now sweating it out of your pores. That is the problem with ramps.

Ramps contain a heady mix of sulfur compounds. As with other alliums, ramps evolved this chemistry to repel pests. Insects avoid the plants, as do many animals (they're toxic to dogs and cats). Humans, however, learned long ago that members of this species have health-boosting properties and add flavor to other foods. In some Appalachian regions, the ramp was called the "spring tonic." It's a vitamin- and antioxidant-rich superfood—the perfect remedy for long winters in a region where fresh fruits and vegetables were in short supply. Just like garlic, ramps boost immunity, lower cholesterol and blood pressure, and strengthen blood vessels. And just like garlic, if you eat enough of the little green devils you will stink to high heaven.

These days, ramps are on the foodie radar. You'll find them on pizzas, mixed with gourmet grits, pickled and tossed with salmon, and you'll even see recipes for ramp jam. But beware. These treatments only partially tame the reek of the ramp.

So if you ever feel the need to be told that you smell like fetid cabbage, rancid garlic butter, stinky feet, rotting fish, or an open sewer, cook up a mess of ramps and enjoy.

Speaking of Socks

Durian is a football-sized fruit with ugly-looking spines. Its flavor poses one of the weirdest contrasts in the culinary world. It smells like unwashed socks but tastes sweet. Imagine eating vanilla pudding while trying not to inhale.

Durian: a tropical treat with a bouquet reminiscent of finely mellowed sewage.

Drink Up!

There are worse things you can do than gulp down urine. In fact, the practice of urine consumption, or *urophagia*, dates all the way back to the ancient Egyptians, Chinese, Indians, and Aztecs, who imbibed in this very personal nectar for health purposes.

It Quenches Your Thirst in a Pinch

Of course, "health purposes" is a relative term. If you're in dire circumstances in which no fresh water is available, drinking urine can supposedly help prevent dehydration. Given that urine is composed mostly of water, the first golden drink may be fairly harmless. If you were to go back to the urine well repeatedly, however, you'd run into the law of diminishing returns—the percentage of usable water in your pee would decrease and harmful flushed waste products would increase.

These harmful substances could include drugs or other chemicals from the environment that exit the body in a hurry via the kidneys, which would take a beating as they continuously tried to recycle compounded toxins. In addition, the high salt content in urine would eventually lead to dehydration, not stave it off.

Urine as a Hallucinogen

However, if it's psychotropic trips you're after, perhaps scoring the Koryak tribe of Siberia as your new drinking buddies would be just the thing. The Koryak tribesmen swig each other's urine to prolong highs after consuming mind-altering mushrooms during rituals.

Some cultures believe that supplemental consumption of urine keeps illnesses at bay. The holistic approach of Indian Ayurvedic medicine known as Amaroli uses urine to treat asthma, arthritis, allergies, acne, cancer, heart disease, indigestion, migraines, wrinkles, and other afflictions. There is no proof that these treatments work, but since urine is sterile (as long as it isn't contaminated with the Koryak's psychedelic mushrooms), it does have antibacterial, antifungal, and antiviral qualities.

Urine Therapy

Some people laud pee as a power-packed elixir brimming with vitamin, hormone, and protein goodness. Apparently, rocker Jim Morrison and actor Steve McQueen participated in urine therapy.

Like most anything, however, moderation is the key. According to the Chinese Association of Urine Therapy, negative side effects include diarrhea, fatigue, fever, and muscle soreness; these problems worsen as you drink more. You may also want to beware if you ever see someone clad in a T-shirt that's emblazoned with the words, "Koryak Chug-a-lug Champ."

When Frog Legs Aren't Enough

Bored with all the traditional ways of getting high: cocaine, marijuana, and Ecstasy? Looking for a new, disgusting, and unhygienic way to tune out for a while? Look no further than the banks of the Colorado River, dude.

Hopping along the river's shores in southern Arizona, California, and northern New Mexico, the *Bufo alvarius* (also called the "Cane Toad" and "Colorado River Toad") would normally be in danger of being the main course for a wolf or Gila monster. That is, it would if it weren't for a highly toxic venom that this carnivorous toad produces whenever it gets agitated: the same venom that can get you high as a kite if properly ingested.

The toad's venom is a concentrated chemical called bufotenine. It also happens to contain the powerful hallucinogen 5-MeO-DMT (or 5-methoxy-dimethyltryptamine). Ingested directly from the toad's skin in toxic doses (such as licking its skin), bufotenine is powerful enough to kill dogs and other small animals. However, when ingested in other ways—such as smoking the toad's venom—the toxic bufotenine burns off, leaving only the 5-MeO-DMT chemicals. Those can produce an intense, albeit, short-lived rush that has been described as 100 times more powerful than LSD or magic mushrooms, even if it takes a lot more work to get it.

As one of the few animals that excrete 5-MeO-DMT, these toads are leathery and greenish-gray or brown. They can grow up to seven inches long. They have four large glands that are located above the ear membranes and where their hind legs meet their bodies. Toad-smokers first milk the venom from the amphibian by rubbing its glands, which causes it to excrete the bufotenine. Then they catch the milky white liquid in a glass dish or other container. After the bufotenine has evaporated, the remaining crystalline substance is collected using a razor blade or other sharp instrument and put in a glass-smoking pipe, and then lit and inhaled. Sounds, uh, fun!

"Toad-ally Tasty?"

CHAPTER 6

If Geography Is So Easy, What Is Wrong with You?

It's one of the great and mysterious failings of Americans: competence in geography. It seems to affect everyone—celebrities who think that New Mexico is the best part of Mexico, presidents who believe Africa is a country, multitudes of average citizens who can't find the capital of their own country on a map—and it's embarrassing. One 2003 survey revealed that the following percentages of young adults couldn't locate these countries on a map:

- Afghanistan: 90 percent

- Iraq: 63 percent

- Israel: 70 percent

- Indonesia: 75 percent

If countries moved around from year to year like athletes on a professional baseball team, then the ignorance might be forgivable. "Syria? I think it was traded to Brazil last spring. Or maybe it was sent down to Antarctica for that import tariff violation." But no. They're in the same locations year after year, sitting there with easy-to-remember shapes. There is no excuse for this. It's a deep flaw in our character.

Meanwhile, members of the animal world fly from one pole to another and swim back to their spawning grounds after years at sea. They don't get lost. They don't even have maps. How do they do it?

How Do Carrier Pigeons Know Where to Go?

No family vacation would be complete without at least one episode of Dad grimly staring straight ahead, gripping the steering wheel, and declaring that he is not lost as Mom insists on stopping for directions. Meanwhile, the kids are tired, night is falling, and nobody's eaten anything except a handful of Cheetos for the past six hours. But Dad is not lost. He will not stop.

It's well known that men believe they have some sort of innate directional ability—and why not? If a creature as dull and dim-witted as a carrier pigeon can find its way home without any maps or directions from gas-station attendants, a healthy human male should certainly be able to do the same.

Little does Dad know that the carrier pigeon has a secret weapon. It's called magnetite, and its recent discovery in the beaks of carrier pigeons may help solve the centuries-old mystery of just how carrier pigeons know their way home.

Since the fifth century BC, when they were used for communication between Syria and Persia, carrier pigeons have been prized for their ability to find their way home, sometimes over distances of more than five hundred miles. In World War I and World War II, Allied forces made heavy use of carrier pigeons, sending messages with them from base to base to avoid having radio signals intercepted or if the terrain prevented a clear signal. In fact, several carrier pigeons were honored with war medals.

For a long time, there was no solid evidence to explain how these birds were able to find their way anywhere, despite theories that ranged from an uncanny astronomical sense to a heightened olfactory ability to an exceptional sense of hearing. Recently, though, scientists made an important discovery: bits of magnetic crystal, called magnetite, embedded in the beaks of carrier pigeons. This has led some researchers to believe that carrier pigeons have magneto reception—the ability to detect changes in the earth's magnetic fields—which is a sort of built-in compass that guides these birds to their destinations.

Scientists verified the important role of magnetite through a study that examined the effects of magnetic fields on the birds' homing ability. When the scientists blocked the birds' magnetic ability by attaching small magnets to their beaks, the pigeons' ability to orient themselves plummeted by almost 50 percent. There was no report, however, on whether this handicap stopped male pigeons from plunging blindly forward. We'd guess not.

Britney Spears is known more for her singing than for her knowledge of geography. Which is probably a good thing, since she's said a few strange things about different parts of the world. For instance, she had this to say about the perks of being famous: "The cool thing about being famous is traveling. I have always wanted to travel across seas, like to Canada and stuff."

And then there was the time she talked about Japan. Or was it Africa? "I've never really wanted to go to Japan. Simply because I don't like eating fish. And I know that's very popular out there in Africa."

And finally, here's what Britney had to say when someone asked her if she would ever want to appear on Broadway: "I would rather start out somewhere small, like London or England."

Continent or Island?

So why is Australia considered a continent instead of an island? In school, some of us were far more interested in the "social" aspect of social studies than the "studies" part. Nevertheless, everyone can recite the continents: Africa, Asia, Europe, South America, North America, Australia, and . . . some other one. What gives with Australia? Why is it a continent? Shouldn't it be an island?

It most certainly is an island (the world's largest) and so much more. Australia is the only land mass on Earth to be considered an island, a country, and a continent.

Australia is by far the smallest continent, leading one to wonder why it is labeled a continent at all when other large islands, such as Greenland, are not. The answer lies in plate tectonics, the geologic theory explaining how Earth's land masses got to where they are today. According to plate tectonic theory, all of Earth's continents once formed a giant land mass known as Pangaea. Though Pangaea was one mass, it actually comprised several distinct pieces of land known as plates.

Over millions of years, at roughly the speed of your hair growth, these plates shifted, slowly drifting apart from one another until they reached their current positions. Some plates reconnected, such as South America and North America, while others moved off into a remote corner like a punished child, such as Australia. (It's no wonder Australia was first used by the British as a prison colony.) Because Australia is one of these plates—while Greenland is part of the North American plate—it gets the honor of being called a continent.

All of this debate might ultimately seem rather silly. Some geologists maintain that in 250 million years, the continents will move back into one large mass called Pangaea Ultima. Australia will merge with Southeast Asia—and social studies tests will get a whole lot easier.

Peary's Journey to the Pole

Robert E. Peary (1856–1920) led an expedition toward the North Pole in 1909. Joining him on the final leg were an African American Matthew Henson (1867–1955) and four Inuit: Uutaaq, Sigluk, Iggiannguaq, and Ukkujaaq.

Why did Peary bring Henson and the Inuit? He had to. Peary was 53, with lots of missing toes, and he mostly rode a dogsled. Whether he reached the Pole or not (and there's reasonable doubt), he couldn't even have attempted the trip without loyal assistance from Henson and the Inuit.

Henson was the ideal polar explorer: self-educated, skilled in dog mushing, fluent in Inuktitut. At one point Henson slipped off an ice floe into the Arctic water, whereupon Uutaaq quickly hauled him out and helped him into dry clothes, saving his life.

Anyone who guesses that Peary got all the credit while the others were ignored wins a slab of *muktuk* (whale blubber). Not until old age did Henson gain some of the recognition he deserved. Though Henson died in 1955, his remains were not interred in Arlington National Cemetery until 1988. Uutaaq passed away a few years after Henson, making Uutaaq the last survivor of the six who at least got near the Pole.

Dissecting Geography

Many a child has hated his or her geography lessons. Even John Spilsbury, an English mapmaker and engraver, recognized this way back in the 1760s. He decided that rather than bore children to tears with rote memorization, he would come up with an interesting and entertaining way to teach them the locations of the countries and territories of Europe and the wider world. Spilsbury used a fine saw to cut apart maps that were pasted onto wooden boards, inventing the first of what he called "dissected maps." They may not have been quite as exciting as episodes of *Where in the World Is Carmen Sandiego?*, but these large puzzles presumably made the subject of geography just a little more bearable for 18th-century children.

How Many People Live at the North Pole Besides Santa and His Elves?

Take a deep breath and relax. Finally someone is going to answer this for you.

The population at the North Pole is as transient as the terrain itself, which is in a constant state of flux due to shifting and melting ice. Human life in this frigid region consists of researchers floating on makeshift stations and tourists who aren't the sit-on-a-beach-in-the-Bahamas type. There are no permanent residents at the North Pole—save, of course, for Santa Claus and his posse.

When you're talking about the North Pole, you're referring to four different locales: geographic, magnetic, geomagnetic, and the pole of inaccessibility. The geographic North Pole, known as true north or ninety degrees north, is where all longitudinal lines converge. It sits roughly four hundred fifty miles north of Greenland, in the center of the Arctic Ocean. The magnetic pole—the point marker for compasses—is located about one hundred miles south of the geographic pole, northwest of the Queen Elizabeth Islands, which are part of northern Canada. Its position moves about twenty-five miles annually. In fact, the magnetic pole has drifted hundreds of miles from its point of discovery in 1831. Then there's the north geomagnetic pole, the northern end of the axis of the magnetosphere, the geomagnetic field that surrounds the earth and extends into space. Last is the northern pole of inaccessibility, the point in the Arctic Ocean that is most distant from any landmass.

If the North Pole were more like its counterpart on the other end of the earth, the South Pole, it would be a lot more accessible. Since the South Pole is located on a continent, Antarctica, permanent settlements can be established. In fact, research stations at the South Pole have been in place since 1956. These bases range in population size, but most average fifteen personnel in winter (April to November) and one hundred fifty in summer (December to March). Combined, the stations house a few thousand people in the summer. The U.S. McMurdo Station alone might exceed a thousand individuals at the peak time of year.

All of this helps explain why Santa chose to live at the North Pole rather than the South Pole. If you're S. Claus and you don't want to be found, there isn't a better place than the North Pole to set up shop, even if that shop is always in danger of floating away.

Get Your Kicks

|||||||||||||||||||||||||||||||||||||||||||||||||||||||||||||||||||||||||||||||||||||||||||||||||||||||||||||||||||||||||||||||||

Route 66 is arguably the most famous highway in the USA, celebrated in history, novels, and songs. As such, it carries a mystique that no modern interstate can surpass. During the 1920s, the American Association of State Highway officials recognized that the country's road system was not advancing at the same rate as automobile ownership. Cyrus Avery, a member of the Association, thought the existing system of named roads (such as the Lincoln Highway and the National Road) was antiquated and should be replaced by an integrated network of numbered interstate routes. He also pushed for an east-to-west route that would stretch more than 2,000 miles from Chicago to California, passing through his home state of Oklahoma. This roadway was formally proposed in 1925. By the following year, it had been approved, allocated the number "66," and opened.

In 1926, much of the highway was still unpaved, but it connected small towns to larger cities, making it easier for rural residents to escape failed farms for better luck in urban centers. As dirt roads gave way to new pavement, a network of motels, diners, gas stations, and oddball attractions sprang up to make long-distance travel along Route 66 not only possible but also comfortable and entertaining.

The Mother Road in American Pop Culture

Writer John Steinbeck was the first to immortalize Route 66 in American culture when he nicknamed it the "Mother Road" in his 1939 novel *The Grapes of Wrath*. Thousands of farmers had left the southern Great Plains region because of the natural devastation caused by dust storms and the financial ruin caused by the Depression. Steinbeck chronicled their situation through the fictional Joad family, who, like their real-life counterparts, packed up everything they owned and hit Route 66 seeking better opportunities in California. After World War II, Route 66 continued its identity as the road to golden opportunities when returning soldiers and their families traveled West to make new lives for themselves.

In 1946, band leader Bobby Troupe celebrated the Mother Road in his song "Route 66," which invited the listener to get their "kicks" by taking to the highway and heading for California. A quarter-century later, the rock band the Eagles paid tribute to Winslow, Arizona—a major stop on Route 66—while extolling the virtues of the open road in their song "Take It Easy."

The roadway's mythic status reached a zenith in 1960 when the television drama *Route 66* debuted. The premise of the series captured the footloose spirit of American youth, following two friends who leave behind the drudgery of the nine-to-five world to tool around the country in a 1960 Corvette, reveling in their freedom while finding adventure and romance on the road.

Beginning in the 1950s, interstates began to replace Route 66, and by 1984, the last part of the original highway was finally bypassed. Sections of the old highway are still maintained as "Historic Route 66," and the spirit of the fabled roadway is embedded in every American who revels in the freedom of the open road.

Actress Raquel Welch was born in Chicago, Illinois. So she should know a few things about it. Like, for instance, the fact that Chicago is a city, not a state. But during one visit to her home city she was quoted as saying: "I was asked to come to Chicago because Chicago is one of our fifty-two states."

The Mother Road begins in either the city of Illinois or the state of Chicago, which is right next to the United States. It ends in Santa Monica, which might be part of Canada.

How Bad Is Your Geography?

Let Us Relieve You of Your Hubris in 20 Questions

So you can recite a few capitals of Europe. Maybe you can find Lake Titicaca on a map. Big deal. This quiz is going to take the starch out of you. Answers follow on page 140. Good luck.

1. This island nation lies only 7 miles off the coast of Venezuela.
A. Tanzania
B. Tunisia
C. Togo
D. Trinidad and Tobago

2. What is the highest mountain range in Mongolia?
A. The Altai
B. The Khangai
C. The Appalachians
D. The Karakoram

3. Which of these lakes is the oldest?
A. Wuhua Hai Lake, China
B. Lake Baikal, Russia
C. Lake Michigan, United States
D. Great Slave Lake, Canada

4. What is the name of the westernmost Aleutian island?
A. Savage
B. Vancouver
C. Attu
D. Last Chance

5. What is the longest river in Australia?
A. Diamantina River
B. The Great Desert River
C. The River Victoria
D. The River Murray

6. Patagonia lies mostly within this country.
   A. Amazonia
   B. Argentina
   C. Latvia
   D. The United States

7. The Dardanelles strait passes through this country.
   A. Turkey
   B. France
   C. Belgium
   D. Portugal

8. Which country contains the Sturt Stony Desert?
   A. The United States
   B. Mexico
   C. South Africa
   D. Australia

9. Which U.S. state has the most lakes?
   A. Minnesota
   B. Florida
   C. Michigan
   D. Alaska

10. What is the highest peak in South America?
   A. Incahuasi
   B. Bonete
   C. Tres Cruces
   D. Aconcagua

11. Which ocean does the Quirimbas archipelago lie within?
   A. Indian
   B. Arctic
   C. Pacific
   D. Southern

12. Which of the following is a landlocked country in Africa?
A. Egypt
B. Mali
C. Cameroon
D. Tanzania

13. Roughly how far is New York City from London?
A. 1,095 miles
B. 2,095 miles
C. 2,470 miles
D. 3,470 miles

14. Brazil borders all of the following countries except:
A. Ecuador
B. Venezuela
C. Bolivia
D. Guyana

15. Which African country is situated on the equator?
A. Nigeria
B. Kenya
C. Guinea
D. Zambia

16. What is the capital of Djibouti?
A. Port Djibouti
B. Djibouti Djibouti
C. Djibouti City
D. Ambouli on Djibouti

17. The Kamchatka region of Russia is:
A. An island
B. An archipelago
C. A metropolis
D. A peninsula

18. Where will you find the Princess Caroline-Mathilde Alps?
A. Austria
B. Switzerland
C. Greenland
D. New Zealand

19. Which of the following is a landlocked country in Asia?
A. Pakistan
B. Iran
C. Laos
D. Myanmar

20. Vaduz is the capital of this country.
A. Latvia
B. Lithuania
C. Liechtenstein
D. Lesotho

Answers

1. D. Trinidad and Tobago
2. A. The Altai
3. B. Lake Baikal, Russia
4. C. Attu
5. D. The River Murray
6. B. Argentina
7. A. Turkey
8. D. Australia
9. D. Alaska
10. D. Aconcagua

11. A. Indian
12. B. Mali
13. D. 3,470 miles
14. A. Ecuador
15. B. Kenya
16. C. Djibouti City
17. D. A peninsula
18. C. Greenland
19. C. Laos
20. C. Liechtenstein

CHAPTER 7

Quick Reads for Quick Stops

Burger King Sets the Bar for Employee Intelligence

Employees of the fast food restaurant in Coon Rapids, Minnesota, received a call one night from someone claiming to be with the fire department. The caller said that the restaurant was pressurized and in danger of exploding, so the employees needed to break all the windows. The amazing part? The employees actually listened and broke multiple windows!

Police are investigating who might have made the prank call.

This isn't the first time a prank caller has targeted a Burger King. In Shawnee, Oklahoma, someone called a Burger King and convinced employees to break windows, claiming there were extremely high levels of carbon monoxide in the restaurant. And a call about a "gas leak" at a Burger King in Morro Bay, California, resulted in $35,000 in damage.

What a Long Strange Trip It's Been Across My Driveway to the Pizza Joint

A Michigan man, Phillip Engle, from Muskegon Charter Township, had a hell of a trip when he was arrested for shooting a gun at a local pizzeria while freaking out on LSD. Not only is that bad, but he was reportedly only wearing a towel and accompanied by his three children.

Engle, who lives near Happy's Pizza in Muskegon, has been known to cause some trouble about town, but this incident definitely breaks all of his personal records. Wearing just a towel, Engle walked to the pizzeria with a gun in hand and began using the butt of the gun to bang on the glass entryway. The glass shattered and the gun then fell and discharged.

An employee at Happy's Pizza reports that Engle was screaming, "No one will help me! No one will feed my kids!" Then, followed by a deep moment of self-awareness, he muttered, "I'm tripping out."

It might seem funny, but the children were awfully scared. Police were called. They arrived at Engle's house where he sat on the porch with a handgun—supposedly a different gun than before. As ordered, he threw the gun into the front yard and then revealed that he had three more guns—that were loaded—inside the house.

While being interviewed, Engle revealed that he had ingested four hits of LSD earlier that day and that he had been having a rough trip. One of Engle's children told officers that he had also shot the dashboard of his car because it wouldn't stop beeping. They found a spent casing and a bullet hole to confirm the story.

Engle was arraigned on four misdemeanor charges: malicious destruction of property, careless discharge of a firearm, reckless use of a firearm, and possession of a firearm while under the influence. Engle will eventually be convicted for bad parenting.

Baggists Are the Sickest

It may be one of the weirdest objects to become the focus of collectors: airsickness bags. People have collected aviation memorabilia since the Wright Brothers, but baggists—those who collect those little paper bags from the airplane seat pocket—are an especially enthusiastic bunch.

Serious collectors, described on the Baggist Hall of Fame website as "those oft-maligned, always misunderstood, but heroic individuals who have taken on themselves the onerous task of preserving the world's bag heritage for future generations," continue collecting their treasures even as airsickness bags are found less frequently on planes nowadays. And the baggist community, just like any other community of collectors, has its own superstars and celebrities. Take Dutchman Niek Vermeulen, for instance, who, as of 2012, had collected 6,290 sick bags from 200 countries to earn a spot with Guinness World Records. And Steve Silberberg, of Hull, Massachusetts, created the Air Sickness Bag Virtual Museum where visitors can browse through almost three thousand different airsickness bags.

One Third of People Agree with Everyone Around Them

In 1953, psychologist Solomon Asch set up an experiment to see how often people conform to those around them. Subjects were told they were being given a vision test, and then asked simple questions with obvious answers. But what the subjects weren't told was that the other people in the room were in on the experiment, and were told to give wrong answers.

With only one subject actually being tested in the experiment, the other "subjects" were used to try to influence the subject's answers by answering the questions incorrectly. One question asked the subject to match a given line with a line having the same length. The answer was extremely obvious, but the sway of the fake subjects' wrong answers led the actual subjects to answer incorrectly as well.

Asch discovered that 32 percent of the subjects gave incorrect answers when everyone else around them also gave the incorrect answers. Even when the correct answer was plainly obvious, nearly a third of the subjects went along with the group.

Asch's experiment showed how social pressure can change opinion—and even change our perceptions of facts! Do people tend to believe obviously erroneous information because many of their peers believe it and tell them it is true? Or can we use our social influence to sway people toward the truth?

15 Awesome Palindromes

Palindromes are words or sentences that read the same backward or forward. Here are some of our favorites.

Go hang a salami. I'm a lasagna hog.

Do geese see God?

Was it Eliot's toilet I saw?

Are we not drawn onward, we few, drawn onward to new era?

A nut for a jar of tuna

Dennis and Edna sinned.

Oozy rat in a sanitary zoo

A man, a plan, a canal: Panama!

Ana, nab a banana.

Borrow or rob?

Vanna, wanna V?

We panic in a pew.

Never odd or even

Madam in Eden, I'm Adam.

Murder for a jar of red rum.

All About *Rangifer Tardandus*

🦆 The word "reindeer" is in no way related to the word "reins." Rather, the Old Icelandic word *hreinn* (meaning reindeer) is the source of the first syllable, but its original spelling was lost in translation.

🦆 Because a reindeer can pull twice its weight for miles over snow-covered terrain, the Saami people of Lapland have used its muscle power for 5,000 years as a primary means of transportation.

🦆 Antlers are made of the fastest-growing tissues know to humans, growing up to an inch a day. Antlers appear within weeks of a reindeer's birth. Regardless of age or sex, every reindeer grows a new set of antlers each year. Antlers are actually bone, while horns are made of keratin, a protein similar to a human's fingernails.

🦆 The secret's out: Reindeer aren't equipped with built-in GPS. Instead, it's their supernatural sense of smell—so keen that they can detect food up to 3 feet below snow—that helps guide Santa's sleigh.

🦆 Blessed with nature's version of an orthopedic shoe, reindeer have wide splayed hooves that distribute their weight evenly. That way, reindeer can walk across snow without sinking, with their hooves working in much the same way as snowshoes.

🦆 The furry layer on a reindeer's antlers is called velvet. Each fall, reindeer rub the velvet off their antlers to signal the rutting, or mating, season.

🦆 If only red-blooded American *Homo sapiens* could be as lucky as reindeer. In the antlered set, the dominant male reindeer called bulls keep harems of females, or cows, throughout the winter for mating purposes. Calves are born each spring, and most cows have one or two calves. Interestingly, reindeer twins are more common in Europe than North America.

Should Auld Acquaintance Be Forgot?

Every December 31, as the clock strikes midnight, English-speaking people all over the world sing "Auld Lang Syne" to herald in the new year. Although few people can claim to know all the words, or indeed what they mean, even fewer know the history of this New Year's Eve tradition.

The song itself dates as far back as the 17th century, but the custom of singing it at the start of a new year didn't begin until the 1930s. Scottish poet Robert Burns first published "Auld Lang Syne" in the mid-1790s, though the earliest mention of this traditional Scottish folk tune was more than a hundred years earlier. Translated from the Gaelic, "auld lang syne" literally means "old long since," but in this context it is better translated as "times gone by." The opening verse of the song asks if old friends and old times should be forgotten. The chorus then answers no, that we should take a drink of kindness and remember the times gone by.

The poignant sentiment and old-fashioned tune are perfect for the dawn of a new year, but it wasn't Burns who transformed the song into a New Year's Eve anthem. The musician Guy Lombardo first played "Auld Lang Syne" a few minutes before midnight at a New Year's Eve party in 1929. He and his orchestra were regulars on New Year's Eve radio (and then television) programs for the next 50 years, and in the process he became that era's version of Dick Clark. Lombardo's New Year's Eve show became so popular that the TV networks CBS and NBC competed over broadcast rights. As a compromise, CBS broadcast the show until midnight, and NBC took over after midnight. This in turn prompted Lombardo to play "Auld Lang Syne" at the stroke of midnight to signal the end of the old year and the start of the new.

Kids Love Crayons

Kids and crayons go together. Crayola claims that the average ten-year-old has already used up 723 crayons, not counting the ones he or she has eaten. A study by Yale University shows that the familiar "crayon scent" is one of the 20 most recognizable smells in the United States.

Smugglers Not Getting Any Smarter

A woman entering the USA was arrested by Customs and Border Protection when her plain-looking burritos turned out to be hiding nearly a pound of methamphetamine.

Susy Laborin was carrying a bag stuffed with what looked like delicious burritos. But when a drug-sniffing dog alerted handlers to a controlled substance, officers found the meth, according to the reports. The meth burritos were worth about $3,000.

Laborin said that she "was supposed to be paid $500 to transport the drugs via shuttle from Nogales, Arizona, to Tucson where she would deliver them to an unknown third party."

Payout from the Golden Arches

Some people are wary of eating at McDonald's because there have been questions about what goes into their food. But Dave Cook, of Chesterfield County, Virginia, found something in his burger that was worth the visit to the fast food establishment. Cook found a $20 bill sandwiched between two pieces of meat on his sandwich.

Cook, who stopped at the restaurant with his mom for a quick bite to eat, was shocked when he found the money hanging from his mouth.

"I've heard of people finding strange things in their salad, but never finding something like this in a cooked burger," he said. "I was in disbelief; I was like 'is this for real?'"

Other patrons began searching for money in their meals, as well, but unfortunately, it doesn't look like McDonald's has started cooking with cash. The managers of the McDonald's have no idea how the money wound up in the burger.

Behind the Mouse Ears

🦆 Since 1967, there's been a private club in Disneyland's New Orleans Square called Club 33. It's the only place in the park where alcohol is sold. Despite a $7,500 initiation fee and $2,250 annual dues, the club has about 400 members and a three-year waiting list to join.

🦆 Until the late 1960s, men with long hair were denied admission to the park. Disneyland had an unwritten dress code and guests were admitted based upon the impression they made on the ticket takers at the front gate.

🦆 When Soviet premier Nikita Khrushchev visited the United States in 1959, he wanted to visit Disneyland, but authorities said they could not ensure his security and denied his request. Instead he was given a tour of Los Angeles public housing.

🦆 Science-fiction author Harlan Ellison was hired as a writer for Disney, but his tenure only lasted a half-day. In the commissary, he joked about making a pornographic Disney film, a comment that was overheard by studio boss Roy O. Disney, Walt's brother, who promptly fired Ellison.

🦆 During World War II, Disney released a series of instructional cartoons for the troops. They also developed an animated film in 1946 called *The Story of Menstruation*, which was used in girl's health classes for several decades.

🦆 Although his fortune was built on the back of Mickey Mouse, Walt Disney was allegedly afraid of mice.

🦆 Until 2000, Disney park employees were not allowed to have facial hair. Now male employees are allowed to sport well-groomed mustaches.

Thinking Outside the Knot

Alexander the Great was a legend in his own time, a bold young king who conquered most of the civilized world. In 333 BC, Alexander, the 23-year-old Macedonian king, was a military leader to be feared. He had already secured the Greek peninsula and announced his intention to conquer Asia, a feat no Greek had yet accomplished. His campaign eventually took him to Gordium, in the central mountains of modern-day Turkey, where he won a minor battle. Though undefeated, he still hadn't scored a decisive victory and was badly in need of an omen to show his troops that he could live up to his promise.

Conveniently, there was a famous artifact in Gordium—the Gordian Knot. Some 100 years before Alexander arrived, a poor peasant rode into the town on his oxcart and was promptly proclaimed king by the people because of a quirk of prophecy. He was so grateful, he dedicated the cart to Zeus, securing it in a temple by using a strange knot that was supposedly impossible to untie. An oracle had once foretold that whoever loosed the knot would become the king of Asia.

Because Alexander was in the neighborhood and had just that goal in mind, he couldn't resist the temptation of such a potentially potent omen of future success. If he could do it, it would be a huge morale boost for his army. Many had wrestled with the knot before, and Alexander found it no easy task. He, too, struggled with the knot as an audience gathered around him. Irritated but not defeated, he decided to approach the problem from a different angle. He realized that if he took the prophecy literally, it said that the person who undid the knot would be king. The legend didn't specify that the knot had to be untied. Deciding that the sword was mightier than the pen, he simply cut the knot in half. It may have been cheating, but it certainly solved the problem.

The prophecy was fulfilled, and Alexander used it to bolster his troops as he went on to conquer the Persian Empire and some of India, taking the title "king of kings."

What Do You Know About Taste Buds?

- Babies are born with taste buds on the insides of their cheeks and overall have more taste buds than adults, but they lose them as they grow older.

- Adults have, on average, around 10,000 taste buds, although an elderly person might have only 5,000.

- One in four people is a "supertaster" and has more taste buds than the average person—more than 1,000 per square centimeter.

- 25 percent of humans are "non-tasters" and have fewer taste buds than other people their age—only about 40 per square centimeter.

- A taste bud is 30 to 60 microns (slightly more than 1/1000 inch) in diameter.

- Taste buds are not just for tongues—they also cover the back of the throat and the roof of the mouth.

- Cats' taste buds cannot detect sweetness.

- The "suction cups" on an octopus' tentacles are covered in taste buds.

- A butterfly's taste buds are on its feet and tongue.

🦆 Attached to each taste bud are microscopic hairs called microvilli.

🦆 Taste buds are regrown every two weeks.

🦆 About 75 percent of what we think we taste is actually coming from our sense of smell.

🦆 Along with sweet, salty, sour, and bitter, there is a fifth taste, called umami, which describes the savory taste of foods such as meat, cheese, and soy sauce.

Stoned, Confused, and Nipped

A man in Texas called police to report that he'd been shot. But it turns out he was just bitten by his dog.

The man had been smoking marijuana on his porch as a thunderstorm passed through the area. Apparently a clap of thunder startled one of his dogs, which then nipped the man in his buttock. The alarmed man then called the police to report the "shooting."

An officer from the Groesbeck Police Department, near Waco, responded and discovered the man had been smoking marijuana and the "shooting" was simply a dog bite. "During the course of the investigation, it was determined that the 'victim' had been smoking marijuana on the porch as the thunderstorm passed through the area," Groesbeck Police Chief Chris Henson said in a Facebook post. "The loud thunder scared one of the dogs causing it to nip the 'victim' in the left buttock. He believed he'd been shot and subsequently called the police."

Henson posted about the incident on Facebook because there had been rumors of a shooting in the area. The dog bite victim was treated at the scene and released.

An Epic Furlough

A man in India last showed up for work in December 1990, but amazingly, he managed to keep his job until January 2015. A. K. Verma, a senior engineer at the Central Public Works Department, was finally fired after twenty-four years of not showing up to his office. Some see this as a sign that India is cracking down on government bureaucrats who avoid office time.

The newspaper *The Hindu* described Verma as being "on furlough," but in 1992, an inquiry ruled against him. Since then, years of delays and inaction have yielded no results in Verma's situation, and finally, he was fired.

"He went on seeking extension of leave, which was not sanctioned, and defied directions to report to work," officials said in a statement.

According to reports, it is not unusual for civil servants in India to show up late to work, take extra-long lunches, or play golf during work hours.

But work attendance began going up when Prime Minister Narendra Modi started cracking down on bureaucrats' behavior. He has been known to show up to offices unannounced, and has instituted fingerprint scanners in offices of civil servants. Since the changes, work attendance has gone up, and Delhi's main golf course is mostly empty during the week.

In This Expert's Opinion

"Louis Pasteur's theory of germs is ridiculous fiction."

—Toulouse physiology professor Pierre Pachet, 1872, on future rabies vaccine creator and germ research pioneer Louis Pasteur

"The abolishment of pain in surgery is a chimera. It is absurd to go on seeking it. Knife and pain are two words in surgery that must forever be associated in the consciousness of the patient."

—French surgeon Dr. Alfred Velpeau, 1839

"Professor Goddard does not know the relation between action and reaction and the need to have something better than a vacuum against which to react. He seems to lack the basic knowledge ladled out daily in high schools."

—*New York Times* editorial, 1921, on future rocket pioneer Robert Goddard

"I see no good reasons why the views given in this volume should shock the religious sensibilities of anyone."

—Charles Darwin, *The Origin of Species*, 1869

"There is not the slightest indication that nuclear energy will ever be obtainable. It would mean that the atom would have to be shattered at will."

—Albert Einstein, 1932. He changed his tune around 1939.

Random Fashion

🦆 Napoleon wore black silk handkerchiefs regularly as part of his wardrobe and steadily won battle after battle. But in 1815, he decided to vary his attire and donned a white handkerchief before heading into battle at Waterloo in present-day Belgium. He was defeated, and it led to the end of his rule as emperor.

🦆 The shoe has historically been a symbol of fertility. In some Eskimo cultures, women who can't have children wear shoes around their necks in the hope of changing their childbearing luck.

🦆 In the Middle Ages, pointy-toed shoes were all the rage. The fad was so popular that King Edward III outlawed points that extended longer than two inches. The public didn't listen, and eventually the points were 18 inches long or more!

🦆 Catherine de Medici popularized high heel shoes for women when she wore them for her 1533 wedding to Henri II of France, who later became king. However, several sources say that men had been wearing heels long before that to keep their feet from slipping off stirrups while horseback riding. A century later, when King Louis XIV of France wore high heels to boost his short stature, the trend became popular with the nobility.

🦆 When Joan of Arc was burned at the stake, she was condemned for two crimes: witchcraft and wearing men's clothing.

🦆 In the 16th century, men wore codpieces for numerous reasons. The frontal protrusions held money, documents, or whatever else they needed to carry.

Greatest Headlines of All Time

"Antique Stripper to Demonstrate Wares at Store"

"Sadness Is No. 1 Reason Men and Women Cry"

"Mayor Says D.C. Is Safe Except for Murders"

"Check With Doctors Before Getting Sick"

"Neighbors Said Sniper Not Very Neighborly"

"Court Rules That Being a Jerk Is Not a Crime"

"Arson Suspect is Held in Massachusetts Fire"

"Enfields Couple Slain; Police Suspect Homicide"

"War Dims Hope for Peace"

"Killer Sentenced to Die for Second Time in 10 Years"

"Two Soviet Ships Collide, One Dies"

"Juvenile Court to Try Shooting Defendant"

"Plane Too Close to Ground, Crash Probe Told"

"Shot Off Woman's Leg Helps Nicklaus to 66"

"Reagan Wins on Budget, But More Lies Ahead"

"Soviet Virgin Lands Short of Goal Again"

"Stud Tires Out"

"Survivor of Siamese Twins Joins Parents"

"Safety Experts Say School Bus Passengers Should Be Belted"

"Fisherman Arrested for Using Wife as Shark Bait"

"Sewage Spill Kills Fish, but Water Safe to Drink"

Pocket Egotism

In 1926, a young Siberian immigrant and inventor named Anatol Josepho created his Photomaton machine, a large booth that could take a photographic image of a person and automatically develop it while he or she waited. Josepho placed his creation in seedy-but-thrilling New York's Times Square. For a quarter, a person received eight photos of themselves within minutes. No one had seen anything like it and word got around. Immediately, the photo booth was a sensation.

People lined up around the block to get their photos taken. In 1932, a Photomaton station opened on Broadway and 47th. Despite the fact that Americans were within the depths of the Great Depression, people gladly forked over a quarter for pictures of family, friends, and even pets.

The photo booth craze continued to rage on; in the 1950s, visual artists such as Andre Breton, Salvador Dali, and Luis Bunuel all took artistic advantage of the photo booth's small and affordable images. Later, pop artist Andy Warhol would also frequent Times Square photo booths.

The chemical-dipped, eight-picture photo booths are no longer manufactured, but there are still many working, old-fashioned photo booths in bars, on fairgrounds, and in various unlikely places around the country. But the photo booth isn't fading away—it's just growing up. If you've been in almost any shopping mall in the past few years, you've probably seen digital photo booths set up in heavy traffic areas. Here, subjects can pick colorful backgrounds and add captions.

Like jazz, baseball, and the quilt, photo booths are a staple of American culture. Call us self-involved if you want, but don't we look great!

The Making of a Jelly Bean

You may not know, and you may not care, but the making of a jelly bean is one enormous process—three whole weeks' worth of work! Candy makers have the sugary treats' creation down to a science, and one thing's for sure: It's not simple.

Most jelly beans start with the inside. Confectioners stir up a boiling mix of flavors and colors to form the inner goo. Some companies even go as far as putting in additions such as real fruit puree. Afterward, it's time to cook up the middle and work toward the outside.

The still-liquid centers slosh to their next step, where machines squirt them out one pop at a time into starch-filled molds. That's where the candies get their shape. After several hours of cooling, the soon-to-be beans are taken out and brushed with sugar. At this point, the candy makers set them aside for as long as 48 hours before moving forward with making the outer shells.

Finally, the beans are ready to be finished. Workers bring the tasty centers into a giant metal rotating pan. There, they shake the beans around for two full hours, letting them gather several layers of external goodness. But the job isn't done yet—the crews still have to pour glaze over the treats to give them their signature shine. A few more days of seasoning, and these little treats are ready to be branded and sent out. Many confectioners use a special kind of food coloring to stamp the company name directly onto the bean. Then machines move the jelly beans into boxes, seal them up for freshness, and finally ship them away—the last step in a long journey from the factory and into your mouth.

Why Is a Football Shaped That Way?

Would you rather call it a bladder? Because that's what footballs were made of before mass-produced rubber or leather balls became the norm.

The origins of the ball and the game can be traced to the ancient Greeks, who played something called *harpaston*. As in football, players scored by kicking, passing, or running over the opposition's goal line. The ball in harpaston was often made of a pig's bladder. This is because pigs' bladders were easy to find, roundish in shape, relatively simple to inflate and seal, and fairly durable. (If you think playing ball with an internal organ is gross, consider what the pig's bladder replaced in some cases: a human head.)

Harpaston evolved into European rugby, which evolved into American football. By the time the first "official" football game was played at Rutgers University in New Jersey in the fall of 1869, the ball had evolved, too. To make the ball more durable and consistently shaped, it was covered with a protective layer that was usually made of leather.

Still, the extra protection didn't help the pig's bladder stay permanently inflated, and there was a continuous need to reinflate the ball. Whenever play was stopped, the referee unlocked the ball—yes, there was a little lock on it to help keep it inflated—and a player would pump it up.

Footballs back then were meant to be round, but the sphere was imperfect for a couple reasons. First, the bladder lent itself more to an oval shape; even the most perfectly stitched leather covering couldn't force the bladder to remain circular. Second, as a game wore on, players got annoyed and were less enthused about reinflating the ball. As a result, the ball would flatten out and take on more of an oblong shape. The ball was easier to grip in that shape, and the form slowly gained popularity, particularly after the forward pass was introduced in 1906.

Through a series of rule changes about its shape, the football became slimmer, eventually assuming its current look. Although it's been many decades since pigs' bladders were relieved of their duties, the nickname "pigskin" lives on.

Old Sparky the Electric Chair

Prisoner Charles Justice was sentenced to death and executed at Ohio Penitentiary on November 9, 1911, courtesy of "Old Sparky," for the crimes of robbery and murder. Now here's the ironic part: Justice had been a prisoner in the same prison in 1900, where he helped clean the area where the electric chair was kept. Originally, the condemned prisoners would be bound to the chair by leather straps; if they strained under them and their skin broke contact with the chair's electrodes, the charge would jump the gap and severely burn their flesh. Justice made the helpful suggestion of using metal clamps to better secure prisoners. His ideas were put to use, and he was paroled for his efforts but ended up right back where he had been 11 years later.

Just Powdering Their Noses

Many modern Americans would be shocked to know how prevalent—and how respectable—cocaine use once was in this country. In fact, one of the most all-American products, the Coca-Cola soft drink, used cocaine in its recipe from 1886 until 1903 and even took its name from the combination of coca leaves and kola nuts. In the late 19th and early 20th centuries, there were no raised eyebrows when doctors prescribed cocaine to patients as a treatment for everything from depression to asthma. The influential psychologist Sigmund Freud made no secret of his own cocaine use, and he urged his followers to try it as well. But after a few decades, it became obvious that the drug led to addiction and psychosis; in 1914, cocaine was outlawed with the passage of the Harrison Tax Act.

Golf? No Sir, Prefer Prison Flog!

That's right—more awesome palindromes!

I won, Karen, an era know I

He stops spots, eh?

Did I draw Della too tall, Edward? I did?

Del saw a sled

A dank, sad nap. Eels sleep and ask nada

Strap on no parts

Won't cat lovers revolt? Act now!

Oh, no! Don Ho

Cain: A maniac

Desserts, I stressed

Lee had a heel

Mr. Owl ate my metal worm

Top step's pup's pet spot

'Tis Ivan on a visit

Straw warts

Roy, am I mayor?

I, man, am regal—a German am I

Evade me, Dave

Bombard a drab mob

Luck of the Irish Bull

An *Irish bull* is a statement that seems to make sense at first, but it turns out to be paradoxical or logically inconsistent upon closer inspection. What is perhaps the canonical example was provided by Professor John Pentland Mahaffey of Dublin University in the late nineteenth century. When asked to explain the difference between an Irish bull and any other bull of unspecified nationality, he said, "An Irish bull is always pregnant." Another well-known explanation of unknown origin regarding an Irish bull says, "Supposing there were 13 cows lying down in a field and one of them was standing up; that would be a bull."

The purest form of an Irish bull is spoken unwittingly (or, even more appropriately, accidentally on purpose). Clearly, Irish bulls are not limited to the Irish. Baseball's Yogi Berra was a master of them, making such remarks as "You should always go to other people's funerals, otherwise, they won't come to yours," "It gets late early out there," and "I never said most of the things I said!" Movie mogul Samuel Goldwyn was another, providing the first known citation of one famous phrase when he said, "I'm giving you a definite maybe." Other bulls attributed to Goldwyn include "Anybody who goes to a psychiatrist should have his head examined," and "We're overpaying him, but he's worth it." Gerald Ford, mocked frequently on *Saturday Night Live* for being clumsy, also stumbled over his words sometimes—as when he said, "If Lincoln were alive today, he'd roll over in his grave."

Oscar Wilde, who *was* an Irishman, probably thought he was merely being witty when he said, "I can resist everything except temptation," but he was also creating a homegrown Irish bull. Examples abound as well in Irish proverbs ("It's better to be a coward for a minute than dead for the rest of your life"). Of course, hundreds of Irish bulls exist, but we'll proceed to stop here.

A pair of cows are grazing together in the pasture. One says, "Heard about this mad cow disease that's going around?" "Yep," says the other. "Makes me glad I'm a rabbit."

June is National Bathroom Reading Month.

CHAPTER 8

Grandpa Did What During the War?

Yes that one. The one with the stain on his pants who sometimes calls you by a former pet's name—he did *that*. And he lived to talk about it. World War II turned average Joes into heroes and made criminals out of law-abiding citizens. It's the source of endless stories, and while you might think that some of them grew in the telling, you'd be surprised by how many madcap improbabilities piled up in those calamitous times.

A few odd things happened to the old duffer.

Audie Murphy

It's striking how Audie Murphy's whole life was really a series of battles. From a dirt-poor childhood to infantryman heroism in Europe to tumultuous personal struggles after the conflict, Murphy seemed ever in a desperate fight. Born in rural Texas, he was the seventh of 12 children. His father left the family when he was 12. Four years later, his mother died. "Getting food for our stomachs and clothes for our backs," Murphy recalled, "was an ever-present problem." Three of his siblings went to an orphanage. Audie Murphy worked picking cotton, and to feed his family, he became an expert at shooting rabbits with a .22-caliber rifle. When the family gathered, he listened raptly to his uncles telling tales of valor during the Great War.

From Pot Scrubber to Combat Hero

When war broke out, Murphy jumped at a chance to join the Marine Corps. But the Marines rejected him. And no wonder—at 18, he was all of 5 feet 5 inches and 112 pounds. He enlisted in the regular army, which, after he swooned during a close-order drill, tried to make him a cook. "To reach for the stars," wrote Murphy, "and end up stirring a pot of C rations. I swore I would take the guard-house first." His ceaseless demands to see combat finally paid off in 1943. Murphy was sent to North Africa, then to the ferocious battle of Anzio in Italy, as part of Company B, 1st Battalion, 15th Infantry Regiment, 3rd Infantry Division.

His upbringing and outlook made him a natural soldier and combat leader. In battle, he preached that a "calm fury" was the best tactic. Under fire, he noted, "Things seem to slow down for me." He shrugged off malaria and a wound in the hip from a sniper's round. By the time his unit invaded southern France in August 1944, he'd earned his first medals and been field-promoted to second lieutenant, a rank he accepted only when assured he could stay with his unit. In one battle, after taking out several machine-gun nests, he lost his best buddy when Germans feigning surrender shot his comrade down. In a fury, he killed the attackers, then turned their machine gun against other strong points. He was awarded the Distinguished Service Cross, the military's second-highest honor.

Murphy's greatest feat occurred on January 26, 1945, during bitterly cold fighting along the German border. His company of 18 was attacked by half a dozen Tiger tanks and over 200 infantry. As his men fell back, Murphy jumped onto an abandoned tank destroyer that was expected to blow any second. He grabbed its .50-caliber machine gun and sprayed bullets toward the Germans while radioing in artillery on himself. "50 [yards] over!" he shouted on the field phone. "50 over?" came the reply. "That's your own position." "Keep it coming!" shouted Murphy.

After single-handedly breaking the attack and killing scores of Germans, he led the counterattack. His actions that day earned him the Medal of Honor. For other feats he was awarded two Silver Stars, two Bronze Stars, three Purple Hearts, the Legion of Merit, and two Croix de Guerre. Of his 37 medals, he sardonically noted soldiers ended up with a "Wooden Cross."

Haunted by War

When Germany surrendered, the men celebrated wildly, but Murphy was desolate. Murphy wrote, "Like a horror film running backwards, images of the war flicker through my brain. The tank in the snow with smoldering bodies . . . . " Thereafter his psyche was stuck in the war. He exhibited the classic symptoms of post-traumatic stress syndrome, then called "shell shock." He wrote, "We have been so intent on death that we have forgotten life."

At home, after welcomes befitting an Achilles, he was wracked with nightmares. Murphy would go to bed armed, sometimes waking up to fire his revolver at the wall. He'd twitch violently and freeze up. Insomnia led to a sleeping pill addiction. His first wife, actress Wanda Hendrix, divorced him. She said he once drew a gun on her. He married again, and with his second wife he had two sons, Terry and James.

Murphy fought his "demons" and helped others with theirs. Ahead of his time, he became an early advocate of aid to veterans returning home with mental health woes. He also bought a house for his sister and found care for his three orphaned siblings.

On to the Silver Screen

After the war, Murphy worked as a rancher and horse breeder. He also wrote country and western songs, some of which were recorded by Roy Clark and Dean Martin. But Murphy channeled most of his pent-up energy into acting. He moved to Hollywood at the suggestion of James Cagney. Training as an actor, he spent penniless years there, bedding on the floor of a friend's gym.

His fortunes changed in 1949 with the publication of his self-penned (with friend Dave McClure) best seller *To Hell and Back*, a terse, savagely honest account of his combat experience. Six years later, the book became a movie of the same name, starring none other than Audie Murphy as himself. The Universal movie grossed $10 million, a record that wasn't broken until *Jaws*.

Best at playing soldiers or outlaws, Murphy also impressed critics in John Huston's *The Red Badge of Courage*. He made a total of 44 films, most of which were Westerns. For his work on the big screen, Murphy was awarded a star on the Hollywood Walk of Fame.

On Memorial Day weekend in 1971, he died at 46 in a plane crash. The craft was manned by an unqualified pilot and had run into dense fog. Murphy was buried at Arlington National Cemetery. Today it's the second-most-visited site at Arlington after JFK's grave.

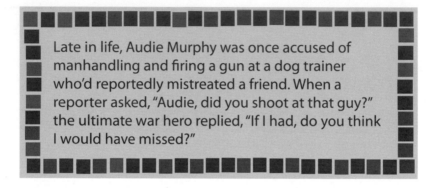

Late in life, Audie Murphy was once accused of manhandling and firing a gun at a dog trainer who'd reportedly mistreated a friend. When a reporter asked, "Audie, did you shoot at that guy?" the ultimate war hero replied, "If I had, do you think I would have missed?"

Merrill's Marauders

The disastrous Allied retreat from Burma in 1942 was a long and arduous ordeal that was part fighting withdrawal and part death march. Lieutenant General William Slim led the remnants of the British Army in Burma 900 miles north into India, battling Japanese troops, deprivation, and disease the whole way. Only 12,000 of Slim's original 25,000 men crossed the border with him. U.S. Lieutenant General Joseph Stilwell marched a ragged group of 114 stragglers a similar distance to India, traveling mostly by foot.

One of the stragglers who accompanied "Walking Joe" was Major (later Brigadier General) Frank Merrill, who two years later would lead his own band of misfits 800 miles back across northern Burma as the vanguard force that would break Japan's grip on the country.

A Schooled Leader

Born in Woodville, Massachusetts, in 1903, Frank Dow Merrill joined the U.S. Army as an underage enlistee, eventually rising to the rank of lieutenant and serving in Haiti and Panama. Initial attempts by Merrill to gain entrance into the U.S. Military Academy were rejected because of his poor eyesight, but he was finally admitted by presidential appointment and graduated from West Point in 1929.

Merrill was subsequently commissioned a cavalry officer and later received a bachelor's degree at Massachusetts Institute of Technology. After a stint as a small arms instructor, he spent three years as an assistant military attaché in Tokyo. In October 1941, he was promoted to major and assigned as a staff officer under General Douglas MacArthur in the Philippines. After Pearl Harbor, Merrill was transferred to Rangoon, Burma, as a liaison officer with the British. He later became General Stilwell's operations officer—just in time to join Stilwell on his walk out of Burma.

A Motley Crew

In January 1944, Stilwell put Merrill in command of a newly formed unit called the 5307th Composite Unit (Provisional). Its role was to perform long-range operations behind Japanese lines in northern Burma. The objective was to reach the town of Myitkyina near the Chinese border ahead of Stilwell's main force and attempt to reopen the Burma Road to China. Code-named "Galahad," the regiment-sized unit would be the first American combat unit to fight on mainland Asia and would become more famously known as "Merrill's Marauders." The Marauders were a hardy, rough-and-tumble mix of jungle-fighting veterans from Panama, Guadalcanal, and New Guinea, who answered a call for volunteers for "a dangerous and hazardous mission." Among them were drunks, malcontents, and violent individuals who were no stranger to the stockade. The unit as a whole didn't buy into regular army routine and discipline, and their behavior was unpredictable at best. There was some trepidation among members of the Allies' Southeast Asia Command about putting Merrill in charge of such a volatile group. He lacked experience in commanding infantry troops. He also had a congenitally weak heart (he collapsed during the retreat to India and had to be carried part of the way), and many questioned if he could handle the strain of guerrilla warfare. But he was optimistic and self-confident, and most important, he knew the Japanese. In the end, he proved to be an excellent choice for leading the mission.

Fighting alongside his men when his heart permitted (other times he was flown to the battles), Merrill led the Marauders across 800 miles of forbidding mountainous terrain and nearly impenetrable jungle in four months. A British officer who witnessed Merrill's command described him as a "cool, clever, and tough fighting man, the type who would never lose his temper or his nerve," and lauded Merrill as a commander who genuinely cared about his men.

The Marauders fought the entire way against the much larger Japanese 18th Division—the same division that had conquered Singapore and Malaya—alternately taking the Japanese head-on or hooking behind them to cut off their communication and supply lines. They spearheaded the way for Stilwell's 23,000 Chinese troops to Myitkyina and capped their remarkable run with the capture of the nearby airfield in May 1944.

In a relatively short period of time, Merrill's Marauders became one of the most accomplished American infantry units of the war, and their extraordinary achievements became the stuff of legend. But the horrific conditions endured by the Marauders took their toll. The unit suffered terrible casualties from fighting and disease; by the end of May, only 200 of the original 2,400 combat (nonsupport) Marauders remained fit for combat. Merrill himself was counted among the casualties after being knocked out of action—but not killed—by two heart attacks and malaria.

In recognition of his admirable leadership of the 5307th, Merrill was promoted to major general and appointed second-in-command of American forces in Burma. He ended the war serving with the American 10th Army in Okinawa and received several decorations, including the Distinguished Service Medal. After the war, Merrill held various senior army staff posts before retiring from the military in 1948. He died in 1955.

"It's Not Illegal if You Don't Get Caught"

Since their country's founding, Americans have generally enjoyed the benefits of a free market economy. During the Second World War, however, the Roosevelt administration realized it would need to control the consumption of many basic goods in order to effectively fight a two-front war.

The World War II-era rationing and price-control system was the brainchild of Wall Street financier Bernard Baruch. He first suggested the scheme in early 1941, arguing that the government should apply rationing vertically (for example, rationing would affect not only automobiles, but also the steel, rubber, and cloth used to manufacture them). To curb inflation, price controls would be needed. Americans would learn to sort through their ration books for items such as gasoline and meat. What Baruch did not take into account, however, was the rise of a vast black market fueled by many ordinary and otherwise law-abiding citizens.

The modern American black market is said to have been born on January 27, 1942. On that day, the Office of Price Administration (OPA) was given authority to enact civilian rationing and price control under Directive No. 1 of the War Production Board. Among the list of items classified as "scarce" were sugar, automobiles, tires, gasoline, and type-writers. Violators could face up to a year in jail and a $5,000 fine, but that was hardly a deterrent. Manufacturers, distrib-utors, retailers, and consumers soon found ways to evade and sometimes profit from the price controls and rationing systems. Consumers learned that with enough money, they could readily find what they wanted—regardless of govern-ment regulations. By some estimates consumer industries such as department stores, meat packers, and leather tan-ners realized profits as high as 1,000 percent during the war.

The subterfuge took many forms: trimming less fat from meat, counterfeiting gas vouchers, processing livestock through unregulated channels, and ignoring rent controls. Counterfeit vouchers, often sold through organized-crime syndicates, were the most common form of black-market exchange. One arrest in Detroit yielded 26,000 counterfeit vouchers that had been sewn into the lining of gang members' coats.

The black market could not have existed, however, if a large number of Americans had not been willing to engage in illegal trade. To most citizens, the transactions seemed so innocuous that they probably never thought twice about the corner gas station owner selling a few extra gallons for a bit more money or their friend the butcher providing them with a larger cut of meat for the same price.

Efforts to enlighten the public did little. In 1944 Patricia Lochridge wrote a piece for *Woman's Home Companion* titled "I Shopped the Black Market." In it, she detailed how homemakers, ministers, bankers, and other average Americans willingly engaged in illegal activity. Realizing the effect of this trade, the OPA launched campaigns that equated purchasing black market meat with doing "business with Hitler." For the most part, however, Americans ignored the pleas of the ineffective bureaucratic agency. In fact, many citizens sympathized with those who were punished for transgressing the price controls.

Many of the items bought through black market channels had their origin in the military, which was where the goods had been funneled. While the penalty for selling goods within the armed services was severe, even the rumors of executed transgressors did little to slow the brisk business. In the final months of the war, cigarettes had more value abroad than any country's currency. Robert F. Gallagher remembers that while serving as an MP in Belgium, he and his friends often used intermediaries to sell their cigarette rations to locals for a hefty profit. Another common form of profiteering involved the illegal sale of currency. Some soldiers claimed to have made thousands of dollars buying and selling foreign currencies in the confusion and economic depression of postwar Europe. Gallagher: "It's not illegal if you don't get caught."

It is nearly impossible to quantify the amount of black market activity that occurred in the United States during the war. Some have claimed that at the height of the price controls, a majority of the citizens of New York engaged in black market exchanges, and 90 percent of the meat being shipped from San Antonio, Texas, came from black market sources. The black market flourished in part because most Americans mistrusted the goods' regulation. Equally important, the OPA was relatively powerless to enforce its controls: Popularly elected officials were reluctant to take measures of which the majority of their constituents would disapprove. Any society that has attempted to overregulate its market has also had to increase its security and monitoring forces. The police states engendered by Nazi Germany, Soviet Russia, and scores of Third World dictatorships did exactly that to secure the sanctioned exchange of goods and defend government property. Ironically, it was the war against Fascism and the police states of Nazi Germany and Imperial Japan that gave rise to regulation in America—and to the black market.

Architects Go to War

In 1942, with war raging in the Pacific and in Europe, the U.S. military in conjunction with Standard Oil Company constructed two villages in the Utah desert. The first was modeled after a typical Japanese worker's village; the second was designed to the specifications of German housing for low-wage workers. The military spared no expense in creating these villages. They hired prominent architects to design the structures. Prison laborers made the edifices in record time. In the case of the German village, wood was imported from Russia, and the buildings were hosed down to replicate the wet Prussian weather. Finally, designers from RKO Picture Studios furnished the buildings in exact detail, from the bedding, linen, and drapes to the paper wall partitions typical of Japanese interior design and bulky furniture characteristic of German working families' homes. When the buildings were finally just right, the army destroyed them using napalm, gas, anthrax, and incendiary bombs. Then they rebuilt them and blew them up again . . . and again.

The site was the Dugway Proving Grounds weapons-testing area 90 miles southwest of Salt Lake City. Created at the request of President Roosevelt, the program's goal was to measure, as accurately as possible, the potential damage from anticipated massive aerial bombing campaigns on enemy cities—in particular, the effects upon the manufacturing segment of the populations. To further this end, the army staff hired two influential architects whose unique knowledge of their respective subjects made them ideal candidates to design mock structures for the tests. Certainly neither man had ever contemplated designing a structure so that it could be immediately destroyed.

Erich Mendelsohn

Erich Mendelsohn was a Russian-Polish Jew from Germany who had interrupted his architecture studies to drive a Red Cross ambulance for the German army during World War I. His modernist designs marked him as a master of steel and concrete structures that used space to make a unique identity for each project. Among his early work is the Einstein Tower, which still stands in Potsdam near Berlin. Persecuted by the Nazis, Mendelsohn moved first to London and then to Palestine. Eventually, he relocated to the United States where he befriended peers such as Frank Lloyd Wright. Perhaps because of his persecution, Mendelsohn was eager to help design the German worker housing for the Dugway tests. He was particularly useful in the design of roofs, which would receive the brunt of any bomb damage. When Germany surrendered in May of 1945, air raids had eliminated 45 percent of German housing.

Antonin Raymond

Antonin Raymond was a Bohemian who had moved to the United States in 1910. In 1916, he worked as an associate in Frank Lloyd Wright's studio Taliesin, in Wisconsin, and aided in the design of the Imperial Hotel in Tokyo. While in Tokyo, Raymond developed a deep fondness for Japanese design—a passion that would last his entire life. Nevertheless, he was amicable when the U.S. Army asked him to design the Japanese village at Dugway. Constructed almost entirely of wood, the mock village burned to the ground after a few tests. Its fate predicted that of real Japanese cities that were bombed during the war. In a single raid upon the paper-and-wood city of Asakua, for instance, 334 B-29 bombers dropped 2,000 tons of napalm, destroying an unprecedented 265,171 buildings.

Citizen Kane Goes South

Brazil began World War II as a neutral nation. However, Roosevelt and his advisers recognized that the country would be an ideal supply point for the anticipated African campaign. Though ruled by a Fascist dictator, Brazil sought to curry favor with the United States and declared war on Germany in 1942. But Brazil's ruler, Getúlio Vargas, had reservations about his country's involvement in the war. He also realized Brazil would be the likely landing spot for German forces attempting to establish a base in the Western hemisphere. As a goodwill gesture, Roosevelt chose a personal friend, *Citizen Kane* director Orson Welles, to go to Brazil and film the country's annual Carnival celebration.

As soon as Welles had left the country, RKO began slashing and refilming significant portions of the company's current Welles production, *The Magnificent Ambersons*. Far away in

Rio de Janeiro, Welles was powerless to stop the damage. Instead, with characteristic enthusiasm, he began producing three short Brazilian films. When money for the project ran out, Welles took to the jungle with a small camera crew and continued to document the country's indigenous culture. Since Welles remained under contract to RKO, the footage, titled *It's All True*, was taken from the young director and never returned. The film was presumed lost until a month before Welles's death in 1985, when it was discovered in a Paramount studio vault.

Though Welles was in Brazil at the behest of the U.S. government, his absence from the studio and failure to finish *The Magnificent Ambersons* burdened him with a lasting reputation as an irresponsible director incapable of finishing a project. For the rest of his career, he struggled to continue making films outside the powerful studio system. Though he succeeded in producing many brilliant films, his craft was compromised by his constant search for funding.

They Got It on Kodachrome

During his 40 years in Hollywood, director George Stevens worked with such actors as Cary Grant and James Dean. He believed that some of his most important work behind the camera, however, was done without a script.

Commissioned as a major in the Army Signal Corps, the Hollywood director and his crew, called "Stevens Irregulars," landed with the U.S. 1st Army on the D-Day beaches. For the next year, they followed troops across Europe. While shooting standard black-and-white film for the Army Motion Picture Unit, Stevens also used 16mm Kodachrome color film for his own "home movies."

Stevens and his crew witnessed the Allied breakout at St.-Lô, the liberation of Paris, the Battle of the Bulge, and the crossing of the Rhine. They also filmed the underground factory at Nordhausen, where slave laborers built the V-1 rockets; the liberation of the Dachau concentration camp; the release of Allied POWs; and the meeting of U.S. and Soviet troops at the Elbe River.

After the war, Stevens went back to California. For decades much of his one-of-a-kind record of the Second World War was never seen. The war, though, seemed to change his style of filmmaking. Known for his light comedies before the war, Stevens turned to more serious dramas, including *The Diary of Anne Frank*. After Stevens's death in 1975, his son, George Stevens, Jr., discovered his father's World War II archive and later used the unscreened color footage to create the remarkable documentary *D-Day to Berlin*, which won three Emmy Awards in 1994.

Bat Bombs Away!

World War II inspired innovation and invention as scientists and engineers from the major powers strove to develop weapons that would provide a winning edge. Many of these innovations are well-known—jet engines and rockets in Germany, for instance. However, those that did not work so well are scarcely remembered.

In the early days of the war, an American dental surgeon from Irwin, Pennsylvania, named Lytle S. Adams conceived an idea while on vacation in the American southwest. He proposed that the United States develop a method for attaching small incendiary bombs to bats and releasing thousands of the flying mammals over Japan. Under his logic, the bats would roost in wooden buildings and explode, causing fires that would spread out of control. On paper, Adams's idea held merit—a typical bat can carry 175 percent of its body weight, and since the Japanese populace would not detect the roosting bats, the fires could spread unchecked.

In the weeks that followed America's entry into the war, thousands of citizens sent ideas for new weapons to the White House, and the bat-bomb proposal was one of the very few that went into development. Approved by President Roosevelt, it eventually consumed a modest $2 million of taxpayers' money.

By March 1943 a team consisting of Dr. Adams and two chemists (one from Harvard, the other from UCLA) had scoured the caves of the southwest in search of the perfect bat species for the project. Although the mastiff bat was larger and the mule-eared bat more common, the team settled on the Mexican free-tailed bat, because it could carry the requisite weight and was available in large numbers (in fact, one colony of free-tailed bats near Bandera, Texas, numbered some 20 to 30 million animals).

Months of testing followed. The creatures were tricked into hibernation with ice, then a small explosive device was surgically attached by a string. The procedure was delicate and required lifting the bats' fragile skin, which was liable to tear if done incorrectly. The prepared bats were then loaded into cardboard cartons, which were parachuted from aircraft and opened at a preset altitude. There were numerous complications, however. Many of the containers did not open or the bats did not wake up and plummeted to their deaths. Still, the bats did succeed in burning down a mock Japanese village. On the other hand, they managed to start a fire in an airplane hangar that also destroyed a visiting general's car. Perhaps for this reason in June

1943, after more than 6,000 bats had been used in tests, the army handed the project to the navy. It was renamed Project X-Ray. The navy eventually handed off the project to the Marine Corps, which determined that the bat bombs were capable of causing tenfold the number of fires as the standard incendiary bombs being used at the time. However, when Fleet Admiral Ernest J. King learned that the bats would not be ready for deployment until mid-1945, he called off the project. Dr. Lytle Adams was bitter about the cancellation of his novel idea. He maintained that the bat bombs could have caused widespread damage and panic without the loss of life that resulted from the use of the atomic bomb.

"Pappy" Boyington and His Black Sheep

It was the evening of August 4, 1941, and Marine Corps aviator Gregory Boyington had reached rock bottom. Stationed in Pensacola, Florida, he was broke, his wife and children had left him, and his reputation for brawling and drinking had eliminated his chances of promotion despite his talent as a pilot.

That night in Florida, he knew that a representative of the Central Air Manufacturing Company was in a nearby hotel recruiting pilots for a volunteer mission in China. Tired of the Marines and lured by the promise of money, Boyington stopped at the bar for a few drinks and signed up.

He trained with the American Volunteer Group (AVG) in China, also known as the Flying Tigers. Led by Claire L. Chennault, the notorious group learned tactics to

180

combat Japan's best pilots. Boyington remained a drinker and brawler, but with six kills, he earned a reputation as a formidable combat pilot as well. However, Chennault had a maverick personality, and his views frequently clashed with Boyington, who eventually left the AVG and rejoined the Marine Corps. He was recommissioned as a major and sent to New Caledonia in the South Pacific, where he mastered one of the service's newest planes, the bent-wing F4U Corsair.

While on convalescence following a leg injury, Boyington learned that the Marines desperately needed to form new Corsair squadrons, and he organized an ad hoc unit comprising pilots and Corsairs dispersed by other units. The pilots' levels of experience ranged from combat veterans with several air-to-air victories, to new replacement pilots from the United States. Many of the pilots that Boyington pooled to form VMF-214 were known for being misfits with reputations for discipline problems.

The group quickly earned the nickname "the Black Sheep." Boyington once famously quipped, "Just name a hero and I'll prove he's a bum." A discipline problem himself, Boyington understood these pilots and trained them using tactics he'd learned as a Flying Tiger. It worked—in 84 days the Black Sheep destroyed or damaged 197 enemy planes.

His men called their leader "Gramps" because, though only in his early thirties, Boyington was ten years older than most of them. The press dubbed him "Pappy," and the name stuck as his reputation grew. Between August and September 1943, Pappy had added 22 confirmed kills and was on his way to eclipsing Eddie Rickenbacker's World War I record of 26 downed planes.

On January 3, 1944, however, Boyington was shot down and believed to be dead. In fact, he was taken prisoner by the Japanese, who, knowing his identity, tortured him and refused to report his status to the International Committee of the Red Cross. His fate was not known until 18 months later, when Boyington emerged from a POW camp. Though the numbers are disputed by some historians, Boyington is officially credited with 28 kills, making him the leading Marine ace of the war. He was awarded the Medal of Honor.

The Dogs of War

Even "man's best friend" was drafted into military service during the war. The four-legged soldiers protected their two-legged comrades. In fact, no patrol led by a war dog was ever ambushed or fired upon without warning.

The use of dogs in war was not new. In ancient times, Romans and Gauls drove packs of semi-wild dogs onto battlefields to attack and terrify their enemies. During World War I, both sides used them as watchdogs and light beasts of burden, among other duties. Then between 1939 and 1945, dogs became sophisticated, highly trained assistants to their masters in uniform. Utilizing their high endurance, speed, and extraordinary senses of hearing and smell, they saved many lives during combat.

Canine Guards, Scouts, and Soldiers

Germany had the largest prewar canine program of any of the belligerents and trained as many as 200,000 dogs. Each concentration camp had an SS dog unit and the animals were trained to attack prisoners, instilling terror. Other canines were trained as patrols or scouts and used in combat. The SS valued dogs, particularly German Shepherds, because they were fast, intelligent, low to the ground, and, with proper training, almost fearless. The *Wehrmacht* used dogs on all fronts, and even provided some 25,000 dogs to its Japanese allies to use in China.

On the Eastern Front, the Soviet Union conscripted breeds like the reliable Samoyed, a hardy Siberian sled dog, to pull light equipment and litters bearing wounded men. Eventually, the Soviet Army formed 168 canine units from a variety of breeds and developed specialized guard breeds such as the Black Russian Terrier at its Red Star Kennels outside Moscow. Some of the Red Star's less-fortunate graduates also included "suicide dogs," conditioned to locate food underneath tanks while carrying backpacks loaded with high explosives.

To the west, Britain and France also recruited dogs for auxiliary duty. In May 1940, as the *Wehrmacht* swept across France, nearly 200 dogs were among the host evacuated from Dunkirk across the English Channel.

Dogs for Defense—Training Canines in the United States

In the United States, patriotic members of the American Kennel Club started an organization called "Dogs for Defense." They called on citizens to donate their dogs to the war effort. The War Department began inducting dogs as service animals in March 1942, assigning them to the Quartermaster Corps. During the war, the U.S. Army, Marines and Coast Guard trained more than 10,000 German Shepherds, Doberman Pinschers, Belgian Sheep Dogs, and other "acceptable" breeds for what became popularly known as the "K-9 Corps."

U.S. services trained their dogs at special centers around the country, including one established on Cat Island near Gulfport, Mississippi. The eight- to twelve-week training course went well beyond teaching Private Rover to "sit," "come," and "stay" on command; dogs acclimated to the sounds and smells of battle, practiced riding in military vehicles, and even learned to wear gas masks.

On front lines and in the rear, U.S. war dogs were assigned a variety of duties, depending on their breed, training, and personality. More than 9,000 dogs pulled sentry and reconnaissance duty. They were especially effective in detecting enemy soldiers hiding in foliage or sneaking up on a camp. About 150 dogs were specially trained for messenger duty, running dispatches under fire between the front lines and military headquarters. Others were assigned to the Medical Corps and performed outstanding service locating wounded GIs. Still others, known as "M-Dogs," were tasked with sniffing out enemy land mines.

Army war dogs proved particularly effective in the Pacific Theater, where dense eye-level vegetation obscured enemy soldiers from the average GI. In an age before infrared sensors and satellite reconnaissance, a dog's senses of sight, smell, and sound were the best tools a foot soldier had for picking out an enemy hiding in the bushes. In just one of many instances, the Quartermaster Department reported that during the marine landings on Bougainville Island in November 1943, "D-Day dogs" ran messages, pointed out

snipers in trees, and sniffed out dug-in Japanese defenders at ranges of over 100 yards, giving the marines time to find cover before enemy guns opened fire.

Canine Heroes

GIs learned to value their dogs, and several valiant animals were awarded company citations for heroism. A few dogs even earned combat medals such as the Purple Heart before the War Department changed its policy to restrict combat awards to humans. One famous German Shepherd named Chips faithfully served the 3rd Infantry Division in every major European and African operation. He wore eight battle stars bestowed by his company's men. In one instance while fighting in Sicily, Chips broke away from his handler and attacked an enemy pillbox by himself, mauling one enemy soldier and forcing the machine-gun crew to surrender. At war's end, the dogs, like their human companions, were repatriated to civilian life. The War Department reconditioned the four-legged warriors to view humans as their best friends, and thoroughly tested them for docility before returning them to their original owners.

Combat Medics

Among all the brave men who fought the war, medics and corpsmen stand out for special notice. When a wounded soldier cried out for help, he knew that he would be attended by someone willing to risk his own life to save others.

Mere seconds are significant after being wounded, and the U.S. Army instructed all soldiers in the rudimentary care of wounds they might receive. "First aid is self-aid," stated one slogan. All soldiers were issued an individual first-aid kit. On being wounded, they were to sprinkle sulfa powder on the wound, take sulfa tablets, apply a Carlisle bandage, and seek help. But for serious injuries or wounds that were incapacitating, soldiers depended on the care of the medical corps. Trained doctors and surgeons were always in high demand. Civilian physicians and senior medical students could enter the army as commissioned officers and go to work at trauma units and hospitals relatively far from the front lines. But with too few doctors to go around, the bulk of immediate frontline care was the responsibility of the combat medic.

Medics or aidmen were soldiers themselves, having gone through much of the same basic training as their fellows in arms before being given additional training in basic wound care. They were not experienced health care professionals, but they were called on to make immediate life-or-death decisions without a minute's warning. They carried aid kits with more resources than the individual soldier packets, including penicillin and pain-numbing morphine shots—the syringes of which would be pinned to the clothing of the victim after being administered, as a warning to the next medic to avoid overdosing. They also faced a wide range of situations beyond the obvious bullet and burn wounds. Soldiers thrown around in explosions suffered concussions and fractures that protruded from the skin. Gastrointestinal problems and vitamin deficiencies were widespread. Medics in the Pacific had to treat men suffering from malaria and more unusual tropical diseases such as beriberi, which caused some men to lose all feeling in their legs.

Medics' duties didn't end there. They had to treat battle fatigue, which was not always viewed sympathetically by a man's fellow soldiers, forcing the medic to play the role of psychologist as well as that of medical doctor. They provided aid to civilians caught up in the war zone, including women and infants. Medics in Europe at the end of the war were some of the first to encounter the horrors of the concentration camps, and tried to treat the victims as best they could. They also treated enemy prisoners of war. The latter group was entitled to care under the articles of war, but rendering aid to them sometimes caused hard feelings among the soldiers who had just been in a firefight with the prisoner.

Medic!

It was in firefights that medics earned their reputation as heroes. When one of his buddies was hit, the medic sprang into action, putting aside his personal fears to perform his duty. Medics were always in the thickest of the fight, since that was where their services were most needed. They crawled out into enemy fire, or even an artillery barrage, to attempt to save a life. A medic's safety depended in part on the theater of war in which he served—the Germans generally respected the symbol of the Red Cross the corpsmen wore and avoided firing on them. One medic even reported he was able to wave at German troops to get them to delay fire while he treated an injured man. The Pacific was a different story, and the medics there felt as if they drew extra Japanese bullets. As a result, many dyed their armbands green to make themselves less visible.

Regardless of geography, medics regularly came under attack, whether intentionally or through the fog of war, and continued their efforts despite the danger. Aidman Thomas Kelly refused to leave his injured buddies when his platoon was driven back by the Germans, crawling on ten separate trips through 300 yards of enemy machine-gun fire, dragging wounded soldiers to safety. Corpsman Robert Bush stayed at a wounded marine's side as the Japanese overran their position. He killed six of the enemy while managing to hold a life-saving plasma transfusion bag high in one hand, continuing to fight even after he lost his own eye. Navy pharmacist's mate John Harlan Willis performed a similar feat on Iwo Jima, where he picked up and hurled back at the enemy no fewer than eight live grenades that had been thrown at him and his patient, only to lose his life when a ninth one exploded in his hand. All three were awarded the Congressional Medal of Honor for their efforts, as were other medics in the war. Their fellow soldiers knew the medic in their platoon might save their lives one day, and their repeated acts of heroism were a frequent source of awe. As a result, they were singled out for special treatment, their buddies sometimes volunteering to dig a foxhole for them or relieving them of other mundane tasks.

"Thank God for the Medics"

Such devotion was made even more difficult by the fact that medics rarely had the satisfaction of observing a full recovery. Their first priority was saving lives. After providing immediate aid, their patients were evacuated to safer areas farther behind the lines, given more care, sent farther back, and so forth. The caregivers had little time to do more than ensure that their patient would be alive long enough to make it to the next caregiver before moving on to the next injured soldier.

Despite the hardships it faced, the medical service performed admirably during World War II compared to earlier conflicts. Injured men who received treatment quickly had a very good chance of survival, with mortality rates around 4 percent—half that of World War I. Although one medic claimed that he thought most of the good he did was psychological, making men feel better just by his presence, many soldiers came home with another opinion. Always ready to put their own life at risk to save others, the combat medic earned the respect and admiration of his buddies and established his reputation as "the soldier's best friend."

Military Matters

1. Which naval rank is the highest?
   A. Captain   B. Admiral   C. Commander   D. Lieutenant

2. Which army rank is the highest?
   A. Lieutenant General   B. Major General
   C. Major   D. Brigadier General

3. When was the U.S. Air Force founded?
   A. 1910   B. 1947   C. 1952   D. 1969

4. An enemy army set fire to the White House during this war.
   A. World War I   B. The American Revolutionary War
   C. The Civil War   D. The War of 1812

5. In what war were tanks first used?
   A. World War I   B. World War II
   C. The War of 1812   D. The Korean War

6. Which marine rank is the lowest?
   A. Lance Corporal   B. Corporal   C. Private   D. Gunner

7. How long did the American Civil War last?
   A. Four years   B. Six years   C. Eight years   D. Ten years

8. What was Veterans Day first called?
   A. Armistice Day   B. Soldier Day
   C. Army Day   D. Truce Day

9. In what year was construction of the Pentagon finished?
   A. 1899   B. 1939   C. 1941   D. 1943

10. Which war led to the most American casualties?
    A. The Vietnam War   B. The Korean War
    C. World War I   D. The American Civil War

Answers

1. B. Admiral

2. A. Lieutenant General

3. B. 1947

4. D. The War of 1812

5. A. World War I

6. C. Private

7. A. Four years

8. A. Armistice Day

9. D. 1943

10. D. The American Civil War

CHAPTER 9

Keep a Sporting Attitude

Golf as it is known today is usually traced back to fifteenth-century Scotland. Similar games involving hitting balls with sticks certainly existed earlier in other countries, but none of those countries had scotch to fall back on after a spate of shanks and duffs. Golf, like all sports, has its own rules, terminology, dress code, and sense of doom. This has led golfing devotees to come up with all kinds of philosophies, witticisms, and civilizing guidelines to cover up the game's seething undercurrent of angst and despair. Here's a short list.

"Golf architects can't play golf themselves and make damn sure no one else can."

—Anonymous

"Golf is the only game in the world in which a precise knowledge of the rules can earn one a reputation for bad sportsmanship."

—Patrick Campbell

"Golf is a game where guts, stick-to-it-iveness, and blind devotion will get you nothing but an ulcer."

—Tommy Bolt

"I'm hitting the woods great, but I'm having trouble getting out of them."

—Harry Toscano

"If profanity had any influence on the flight of the ball, the game would be played far better than it is."

—Horace Hutchinson

"There is one essential only in the golf swing: the ball must be hit."

—Sir Walter Simpson

"No, sir. We couldn't 'ave a coincidence like that."

—A Scottish caddie, on being told he was the worst caddie in the world

"Baseball players quit playing and they take up golf. Basketball players quit, take up golf. Football players quit, take up golf. What are we supposed to take up when we quit?"

—George Archer

"It's good sportsmanship not to pick up lost golf balls while they are still rolling."

—Mark Twain

Mark Twain defined golf as "a good walk spoiled."

Like golf, baseball is a sporting endeavor that attracts superstition and fatalism. People build life philosophies upon the game. Compulsive spitting habits too. In their attempts to bring the awful mystery of this pastime down to human level, players and managers have inflicted all manner of wise observations, corny platitudes, and non sequiturs upon us. Some examples:

"You can see a lot just by observing."

—Yogi Berra

"Baseball is 90 percent mental. The other half is physical."

—Yogi Berra

"You don't realize how easy this game is until you get up in that broadcasting booth."

—Mickey Mantle

"You spend a good piece of your life gripping a baseball and in the end it turns out that it was the other way around all the time."

—Jim Bouton

"I have a darn good job, but please don't ask me what I do."

—Stan Musial

"Show me a good loser, and I'll show you an idiot."

—Leo Durocher

"Just take the ball and throw it where you want to. Throw strikes. Home plate don't move."

—Satchel Paige

"I never questioned the integrity of an umpire. Their eyesight, yes."

—Leo Durocher

"When a pitcher's throwing a spitball, don't worry and don't complain, just hit the dry side."

—Stan Musial

Golf and baseball entertain us with their contrasting sides of supreme physical control and flashes of irrationality. Tennis offers a different kind of spectacle: the temper tantrum. Despite the game's genteel history and dapper outfits, players sometimes unravel in epic ways. Here are five of our favorite meltdowns.

John McEnroe vs. Tom Gullikson—Wimbledon, 1981:
The New York Times once dubbed McEnroe "the worst advertisement for our system of values since Al Capone," so it's only fitting his name should appear (twice) on this list. In addition to his usual repertoire of ranting, raving, and racquet launching, McEnroe immortalized his rebellious reputation by continuously shouting, "You cannot be serious!" at umpires and line judges. This behavior continued throughout the duration of the tournament, and despite winning the prestigious prize for the first time, McEnroe was not offered a membership to the All-England club, an honor usually afforded to every first-time victor.

John McEnroe vs. Mikael Pernfors—Australian Open, 1990: Johnny Mac should have boned up on the rulebook before unleashing one of his patented temper tantrums. In his fourth-round match against Pernfors, McEnroe was issued a warning by umpire Gerry Armstrong for intimidating a lineswoman. Later, after he was docked a point for smashing a racket, McEnroe fired off a volley of vindictive vituperations toward the official. Unaware that a new "three strikes you're out" rule had recently been inserted into the code of conduct, McEnroe was rightfully disqualified from further play, and the match was awarded to Pernfors.

Jeff Tarango vs. Alexander Mronz—Wimbledon, 1995:
Talk about mixed doubles! During his third-round match against Alexander Mronz, tennis menace Jeff Tarango put on a legendary display of spoiled sportsmanship, childlike insolence, and all-round bad judgment. After chair umpire Bruno Rebeuh ruled against him on several close line calls, the feisty Tarango refused to continue the match, demanded that the accumulated throng watching the debacle "shut up," and accused the umpire of being "one of the most corrupt officials in the game." At least one denizen in the crowd supported Tarango's view of the proceedings.

His wife, Benedictine, strolled up to the on-court official and delivered an overhand smash of her own. She slapped the official twice across the face before storming out of the arena with her husband, who became the first player in Wimbledon history to default a match because of a disagreement over an official's judgment. Tarango was fined a record $15,500 for his tempestuous tirade.

Serena Williams vs. Jennifer Capriati—U.S. Open, 2004: When her cross-court backhand was ruled out by chair umpire Mariana Alves, Williams was stunned but certainly not silent. She unleashed a barrage of uncomplimentary comments and emphasized her perspective on the proceedings by putting a ball on the court, pointing at it, and pouting. Williams went on to lose the match, and Alves did not umpire again during the tournament.

Greg Rusedski vs. Andy Roddick—Wimbledon, 2003: When a fan in the stands yelled "out" after a Roddick shot, Rusedski stopped playing the point, believing the call had come from chair umpire Lars Graff. After the official refused Rusedski's request that the point be replayed, Rusedski launched into an expletive-laced tirade that even commentator John McEnroe found offensive. The bitter Rusedski went on to lose in straight sets and stormed off the court, refusing to shake the official's hand.

The Slightly Off Line Between Sporting Edge and Malfeasance

Unsportsmanlike behavior, cheating, throwing the game, bending the rules—get used to it. A bit of cork in the bat, a bit of rocket fuel in the veins, a bit of truck exhaust piped into the opponents' locker room . . . every generation of maniacally competitive athletes adds its own wrinkle. But it's not just the athletes to watch out for. You need to keep an eye on those crafty little groundskeepers too.

"A good groundskeeper can be as valuable as a .300 hitter," owner Bill Veeck once said. He would have known. Veeck's head groundskeeper was Emil Bossard, who spawned a legacy that has helped keep the "home" in home field advantage. Bossard had a big job in Cleveland from the 1930s to the 1950s as caretaker for League Park and Municipal Stadium, the two fields used by the Indians at the time. He built the mound tall when fireballer Bob Feller pitched, and he kept the grass on the left side thick, as player-manager Lou Boudreau requested. When slugging clubs like the Yankees came in, the outfield grass was left especially long and wet to turn their doubles into singles. And that's not all. Years later, Roger Bossard confessed that his grandfather used to move the portable fence back 10 to 15 feet against the Yankees to diminish their power. Interestingly enough, Cleveland was the only American League team to win multiple pennants during the Yankees' run from 1941 to '64.

The Bossards branched out. Harold and Marshall took over in Cleveland for their father. Brother Gene went to Chicago's Comiskey Park, where the club won its first pennant in 88 years with Veeck and Bossard having a hand in things. Gene watered down the field—earning Comiskey the nickname of "Camp Swampy"—and kept baseballs in a freezer to cut down on home runs by slugging opponents. Grandson Roger maintains Comiskey's successor (Guaranteed Rate Field) and claims to be one of the last groundskeepers to know the special maneuvers used by previous generations. "I won't let the tricks die," he told the Sports Turf Managers Association. ESPN listed the Bossard family as number seven on the all-time list of baseball cheaters.

Other groundskeepers took to drowning the field to help ensure victory. During the 1962 best-of-three playoff between the San Francisco Giants and Los Angeles Dodgers, Candlestick Park groundskeeper Matty Schwab stepped in to give his players an edge. At the behest of Giants manager Alvin Dark, the ground was soaked around first base to slow Dodgers speedster Maury Wills. While umpire Jocko Conlan made Schwab work to dry out the right side of the infield, the left side went untouched and remained a sponge to slow down grounders. The Giants won the game (Wills never reached base), and shortstop Joe Pagan fielded eight chances flawlessly. The Giants went on to win the pennant. Schwab, who'd been lured from the Dodgers to the Giants back when the teams were in New York, received a full World Series share. Dark would forever retain the nickname "Swamp Fox."

But Schwab was not alone in his tactics. The Tigers grounds crew would regularly drench the area around home plate to help Ty Cobb's bunts stay fair. The Indians watered down third base to protect Al Rosen, who broke his nose nine times while fielding ground balls. And the Kansas City groundskeeper George Toma, among others, wet the mound and then let it bake in the sun when the opposing pitcher was Catfish Hunter, who preferred a soft mound.

Speaking of Unfair Advantages

So why do batters cork their bats anyway? Are there really any benefits?

There are different ways to cork a wooden baseball bat, but the basic procedure goes like this: Drill a hole into the top of the bat, about an inch in diameter and twelve inches deep; fill the hole with cork—in rolled sheets or ground up—and close the top with a wooden plug that matches the bat; finally, stain and finish the top of the bat so that the plug blends in.

The supposed benefits of a corked bat involve weight and bat speed. Cork is lighter than wood, which enables a player to generate more speed when swinging the bat. The quicker the swing, the greater the force upon contact with the ball—and the farther that ball flies. The lighter weight allows a batter more time to evaluate a pitch, since he can make up the difference with his quicker swing; this extra time amounts to only a fraction of a second, but it can be the difference between a hit and an out at the major league level.

Following the logic we've set forth, replacing the wood in the bat with nothing at all would make for an even lighter bat and, thus, provide more of an advantage. The problem here is that an empty core would increase the likelihood that the bat would break; at the very least, it would cause a suspicious, hollow sound upon contact with the ball. The cork fills in the hollow area, and does so in a lightweight way.

Not everyone believes that a corked bat provides an advantage; some tests have indicated that the decreased bat density actually diminishes the force applied to the ball. But Dr. Robert Watts, a mechanical engineer at Tulane University who studies sports science, sees things differently. He concluded that corking a bat increases the speed of the swing by about 2.5 percent; consequently, the ball might travel an extra fifteen to twenty feet, a distance that would add numerous home runs to a player's total over the course of his career.

In any case, we haven't heard much lately about corked bats. That's because the headlines have been dominated by players who have used steroids to cork themselves.

Bill Klem: Greatest Umpire of All Time

Try to start a discussion that begins, "Who was the greatest [blank] of all time?" and you'll be in for some argument—unless the blank is "umpire." In that case, the answer is unquestionably Bill Klem. He was so good, and it was so obvious that he was so good, that for 16 of his record-setting 37-year National League career he only umpired behind the plate. That wasn't a reward for years of quality service—it started the first day he umped in the major leagues. He was uniquely skilled at calling balls and strikes.

Klem wasn't large, but he commanded respect because of his hard work and integrity. He took grief from some of the game's legendary grief-givers, but when the heat got to be too much, Klem would draw a line in the dirt with his toe, announce, "Don't cross the Rio Grande," and turn his back. Anyone who crossed that line was headed for the showers. He was often called "The Old Arbitrator," and that nickname (which Klem loved) is on his Hall of Fame plaque. But if you called him "Catfish" (because of his looks), you were tossed immediately.

Klem pioneered the inside chest protector, which allowed for a better view of the pitch than the protectors that were previously worn outside the shirt. And he was one of the first to use hand signals for strikes and fouls. He umpired 104 World Series games in 18 Series—almost twice as many Series as any other ump—and he worked at the first All-Star Game in 1933. When he retired in 1941 at age 67, he was the oldest ump in baseball history.

Klem did one very important thing that many umpires never do, although they should: wait. He would hesitate and let the facts clarify themselves in his mind before making a call. Once when Klem paused before signaling safe or out, the frustrated catcher shouted, "Well, what is he?" Klem answered, "He ain't nothing till I call it."

Dribbling Drivel

There are numerous rules on how to properly dribble a basketball, but bouncing the ball with such force that it bounds over the head of the ball handler is not illegal. Although it might fun-up the standard NBA game to see players drumming dribbles with the exaggerated effort of the Harlem Globetrotters, it wouldn't do much to move the game along. And contrary to popular belief, there is no restriction on how high a player may bounce the ball, provided the ball does not come to rest in the player's hand.

Anyone who has dribbled a basketball can attest to the fact it takes a heave of some heft to give the globe enough momentum to lift itself even to eye-level height. Yet, the myth about dribbling does have some connection to reality. When Dr. James Naismith first drafted the rules for the game that eventually became known as basketball, the dribble wasn't an accepted method of moving the ball. In the game's infancy, the ball was advanced from teammate to teammate through passing. When a player was trapped by a defender, it was common practice for the ball carrier to slap the sphere over the head of his rival, cut around the befuddled opponent, reacquire possession of the ball, and then pass it up court. This innovation was known as the overhead dribble, and it was an accepted way to maneuver the ball until the early part of the 20th century. The art of "putting the ball on the floor" and bouncing it was used first as a defensive weapon to evade opposing players.

By the way, there is absolutely no credence to wry comments made by courtside pundits that the "above the head" rule was introduced because every dribble that former NBA point guard Muggsy Bogues took seemed to bounce beyond the upper reaches of his diminutive 5'3" frame.

The Hidden History of the Jockstrap

On November 28, 2005, the Bike Athletic Company celebrated the production of its 350 millionth jockstrap, which was promptly framed and flown to the company's headquarters. Lets take a closer look at some landmarks in the long history of this piece of men's protective underwear.

The Birth of a Legend

The origin of the jockstrap begins in 1874, thanks to Charles Bennett, who worked for the Chicago-based sporting goods company Sharp & Smith. Originally, Bennett designed his garment to be used by bicyclists in Boston. In 1897, Bennett and his newly formed BIKE Web Company (as Bike Athletic was known then) officially patented his invention. At the time, a bicycle craze was sweeping the nation. These bikes weren't like today's average cruisers; instead, the bicycles of yore were high-wheeled and quite precarious. Folks raced these bikes around steeply banked velodrome tracks as well as through Boston's bumpy cobblestone streets. The daredevils on the velodromes were known as "bike jockeys," which led to Bennett naming his invention the "BIKE Jockey Strap," later shortened to "jockstrap." Two decades later, the U.S. Army issued jockstraps to World War I soldiers in order to reduce "scrotal fatigue." When the troops came home, the bicycle craze had been replaced by the rough and tumble sport of football; the jockstrap found a new home on the gridiron.

Entering Manhood Via the Locker Room

To most men of a certain age, the jockstrap is a right of passage that signals the arrival of puberty and a need to protect the male reproductive organs during vigorous exercise. To the uninitiated (or female), the jockstrap might contain some mystery, but its construction is rather simple.

A jockstrap (or athletic supporter) consists of an elastic waistband and leg straps connected to a pouch that holds the testicles and penis close to the body, sometimes with the added plastic cup (ostensibly to avoid injury). The original design, with the addition of the cup, hasn't changed much since the early 1900s.

A Milestone Missed

When the jockstrap turned 100 years old in 1974, the anniversary passed quietly—alas, no national magazine covers commemorating the garment, no ticker-tape parade. Perhaps it was due to a national feeling of modesty, yet 15 years later, as a journalist writing for the *Orlando Sentinel* remarked, a certain women's undergarment—the bra—received plenty of press for its centennial. In fact, when the bra turned 100, *Life* magazine issued six pages to celebrate, along with a pictorial, and a headline shouting "Hurrah for the bra." Ten years later, as the jockstrap turned 125, a *Houston Chronicle* writer wondered why we'd forgotten about the forsaken jockstrap. Perhaps we'd been too distracted by Y2K in 1999, he wrote, or maybe "the jock just isn't in the same league [as the bra]. A bra suggests female mystery; a jock suggests male vulnerability."

The Decline of the Jock?

In the past few decades, there has been some run on jockstrap territory by the likes of the more free-flowing boxer shorts, jockey shorts, and, for athletic types, "compression shorts." Slowing numbers can be pointed to increased competition, or perhaps men are acting out against years of ridicule by classmates and less-than-tactful gym teachers. Still, after more than 130 years on the market, the jockstrap probably isn't going anywhere just yet.

Saving Face: The Hockey Goalie Mask

Gruesome facial injuries to two legendary hockey goalies spurred the invention and acceptance of the goalie mask. Yet despite the hazards posed by playing without a mask, the face-saving innovation took a long time to catch on.

On April 7, 1974, the Pittsburgh Penguins faced off against the Atlanta Flames as the 1973–74 National Hockey League regular season drew to a close. Playing in goal for the Penguins was a 30-year-old journeyman named Andy Brown.

Brown turned in a sievelike performance, and the sad-sack Penguins were thrashed 6–3. Worse yet, the loss turned out to be the last game of Brown's NHL career. But as he braved face-mashing pucks whizzing past his head, Brown staked his place in hockey history: He would be the last goalie to ever play in an NHL game without a goalie mask.

Today, it's hard to fathom how a hockey goalie could play without his mask. Indeed, both pro and amateur hockey leagues now require the mask to be a part of a goalie's equipment. But for the first nine decades of professional hockey's existence, the goalie mask was an object as odd and rare as the U.S. two-dollar bill.

As insane as it sounds, most goalies actually chose not to wear any protective face gear, despite the obvious occupational hazards. Not surprisingly, then, the introduction and popularization of the goalie mask only came about after a near-tragedy involving two of the game's greatest netminders.

Clint Benedict played 18 pro seasons with the Ottawa Senators and Montreal Maroons, backstopping the Senators to Stanley Cup titles in 1920, 1921, and 1923, as well as helping lead the Maroons to their first Cup win in 1926. Arguably the best goalie of his era, Benedict revolutionized how the position was played. He earned the nickname "Praying Benny" due to his habit of falling to his knees in the era of the stand-up goaltender. As a result, the NHL eventually abandoned its rule prohibiting goalies to leave their feet.

In 1930, Benedict inadvertently contributed to yet another innovation to the goal-tending profession. That year, in a game between the Maroons and the Montreal Canadiens, the Canadiens' Howie Morenz nailed Benedict in the face with a shot that knocked him completely unconscious, shattered his cheekbone and nose, and hospitalized him for a month. When Benedict returned to the ice to face the New York Americans, he surprised the crowd by sporting a leather mask, making history as the first goalie to wear face protection in an NHL game.

After five games, Benedict fatefully discarded the mask, saying its oversize nosepiece hindered his vision. Shortly after, another Morenz shot struck Benedict in the throat and ended his NHL career. Amazingly, for the next 29 years, the first man to wear a mask in a game would also be the last.

The mask finally made its reappearance in 1959—albeit unexpectedly—in a game between the Montreal Canadiens and the New York Rangers. Three minutes into the game, Rangers star Andy Bathgate drilled the Canadiens' all-star goalie Jacques Plante in the nose and cheek with a hard shot, sending a badly bleeding Plante to the dressing room.

Plante had been wearing a fiberglass mask in practices since the mid-1950s, but Montreal coach Toe Blake forbade him to don it in a game. Now, as Plante was being stitched up, he told the coach he wouldn't go back on the ice without his mask. An irate Blake, faced with no suitable backup goalie, was forced to relent.

Plante returned to the game wearing his mask and led the Canadiens to a 3–1 victory. Montreal subsequently reeled off an 18-game unbeaten streak, with a masked Plante in net for every game. The goalie mask was here to stay.

Within a decade, the mask became commonplace throughout hockey. By 1974, all NHL goalies wore a mask. Except, of course, for Andy Brown.

Out in Left Field

1. In golf, the mulligan refers to this action.
   A. Landing the ball in a sand trap
   B. Taking a free, or do-over shot
   C. Deliberately aiming at another player
   D. Coughing loudly as a player swings

2. What are hockey pucks made of?
   A. Polycarbonate and rubber
   B. Silicone
   C. Shellac
   D. Vulcanized rubber

3. What's at the very center of a baseball?
   A. Liquid encased in rubber
   B. Compressed yarn
   C. Rubber or cork
   D. Leather

4. In the beginning, basketball used these as scoring baskets.
   A. Lobster crates
   B. Whiskey barrels
   C. Peach baskets
   D. Spitoons

5. How wide is a professional football field?
   A. 53 1/3 yards
   B. 35 yards
   C. 50 yards
   D. 35 1/5 yards

6. What is the highest total single-game score in NHL history?
   A. 21 goals
   B. 17 goals
   C. 27 goals
   D. 19 goals

7. What is a cricket bat traditionally made from?
   A. Willow wood
   B. Sealed cork
   C. Laminated pine wood
   D. Ovangkol wood

8. How many foul balls is a hitter allowed in an at-bat?
   A. It's the umpire's decision
   B. Up to 10, if they're consecutive
   C. 3
   D. There is no limit

9. Where does the sport of rugby take its name from?
   A. The town of Rugby, Wales
   B. The town of Rugby, Scotland
   C. Rugby School, England
   D. The phrase "rogue ball"

10. How many minutes of playing time does a hockey game have?
   A. 90
   B. 45
   C. 60
   D. 100

Answers

1. B. Taking a free, or do-over shot

2. D. Vulcanized rubber

3. C. Rubber or cork

4. C. Peach baskets

5. A. 53 1/3 yards

6. A. 21 goals

7. A. Willow wood

8. D. There is no limit

9. C. Rugby School, England

10. C. 60

CHAPTER 10

Who Was That Shadowy Figure?

The underworld of espionage—it's a world of coded messages, questionable identities, and faked evidence. It also has some really cool jargon. Here are 11 terms used by spies.

1. Black Bag Job

A black bag job, or black bag operation, is a covert entry into a building to plant surveillance equipment or find and copy documents, computer data, or cryptographic keys. The name is derived from the black bags spies used to carry the equipment for such operations. In 1972, the Supreme Court declared black bag jobs unconstitutional. Are bags of different colors okay?

2. Brush Contact

A brush contact is a brief and public meeting in which two spies discreetly exchange documents, funds, or information without speaking to each other, except perhaps to utter "Excuse me" or other pleasantries. To the average person, the interaction would seem like an accidental encounter between two strangers.

3. L-Pill

An L-pill is a lethal pill carried by spies to prevent them from revealing secrets if captured and tortured. During World War II, some L-pills contained a lethal dose of cyanide encased in a glass capsule that could be concealed in a fake tooth and released by the agent's tongue. If he bit into the capsule and broke the glass, death would be immediate.

But if the pill came loose and was swallowed accidentally while the agent was sleeping or chewing gum, it would pass through his system without causing any harm, as long as it didn't break and release the poison.

4. Window Dressing
The best spies are able to blend into any situation. To accomplish this, they use window dressing—the cover story and accessories they use to convince any authorities and casual observers that they are everyday people and not spies. For example, if a spy is impersonating a construction worker to cover the fact that he is planting a listening device, his window dressing might include official-looking work orders, tools, and knowledge of the people who would have authorized his presence.

5. Sheep Dipping
In farming, sheep dipping is a chemical bath given to sheep to rid them of any bugs or disease or to clean their wool before shearing. In CIA terminology, sheep dipping means disguising the identity of an agent by placing him within a legitimate organization. This establishes clean credentials that can later be used to penetrate adversary groups or organizations. Similar to the real sheep, the agent is cleaned up so that nobody knows where he's been, kind of like money laundering.

6. Canary Trap
Do you suspect a leak in your organization? Even if the leakers aren't small yellow birds, you might be able to catch them by setting a canary trap—giving different versions of sensitive information to each suspected leaker and seeing which version gets leaked. Although this method has been around for years, the term was popularized by Tom Clancy in the novel *Patriot Games*.

7. Dangle

In spy terminology, a dangle is an agent who pretends to be interested in defecting to or joining another intelligence agency or group. The dangle convinces the new agency that they have changed loyalties by offering to act as a double agent. The dangle then feeds information to their original agency while giving disinformation to the other.

8. Honeypot

A honeypot is a trap that uses sex to lure an enemy agent into disclosing classified information or, in some cases, to capture or kill them. In the classic Hitchcock film *North by Northwest*, Eva Marie Saint's character was both a honeypot and a double agent. In real life, in 1961, U.S. diplomat Irvin Scarbeck was blackmailed into providing secrets after he was lured by a female Polish agent and photographed in a compromising position.

9. Camp Swampy

Camp Swampy is the nickname of the CIA's secret training base. That's about all that is known about it, except that it was named for the Camp Swampy in the *Beetle Bailey* comic strip.

10. Uncle

Uncle is a slang term referring to the headquarters of any espionage service. One such headquarters is the United Network Command for Law and Enforcement or U.N.C.L.E., the headquarters on the 1960s spy series *The Man from U.N.C.L.E.*, starring Robert Vaughn, David McCallum, and Leo G. Carroll.

11. Starburst Maneuver

How does a spy lose someone who is tailing him? One way is by employing a starburst maneuver—a tactic in which several identical looking vehicles suddenly go in different directions, forcing the surveillance team to quickly decide which one to follow. A classic example of this strategy was utilized in the 2003 film *The Italian Job*. Similar-looking agents can also be used instead of vehicles. Kids, don't try this with your parents.

The Real "Man Who Never Was"

When a drowned corpse washed ashore in Spain holding a briefcase of plans to invade Sardinia and Greece, the Nazis thought they'd made an astounding catch. They couldn't have been more wrong.

The rough tides slapped against the southern Spanish coast in the spring of 1943, carrying the mangled corpse of a British major who appeared to have drowned after his airplane crashed into the sea. The body was just one of the thousands of military men who had met their end in the Mediterranean waters. It floated atop a rubber life jacket as the current drifted toward Huelva, Spain. With a war raging in Tunisia across the sea, a drifting military corpse was not such an unusual event.

But this corpse was different, and it drew the immediate attention of Spanish authorities sympathetic to German and Italian Fascists. Chained to the corpse was a briefcase that happened to be filled with dispatches from London to Allied Headquarters in North Africa concerning the upcoming Allied invasions of Sardinia and western Greece. The information was passed on to the Nazis, who accepted their apparent stroke of good luck, and now anticipated an Allied strike on the "soft underbelly of Europe."

Unfortunately for them, the whole affair was a risky, carefully contrived hoax.

Rigging the "Trojan Horse"

Operation Mincemeat was conceived by British intelligence agents as a deception to convince the Italians and Germans that the target of the next Allied landings would be somewhere other than Sicily, the true target. To throw the Fascists off the trail, British planners decided to find a suitable corpse—a middle-aged white male—put the corpse in the uniform of a military courier, and float the corpse and documents off the coast of Huelva, Spain, where a local Nazi agent was known to be on good terms with local police.

The idea of planting forged documents on a dead body was not new to the Allies. In August 1942, British agents planted a corpse clutching a fake map of minefields in a blown-up scout car. The map was picked up by German troops and made its way to Rommel's headquarters. He obligingly routed his panzers away from the "minefield" and into a region of soft sand, where they quickly bogged down.

This deception, however, would be much grander. If the planted documents made their way up the intelligence chain, Hitler and Mussolini would be expecting an invasion far from the Sicilian coast that Generals Eisenhower, Patton, and Montgomery had targeted for invasion in July 1943.

The Making of a Major

Operation Mincemeat, spearheaded by Lieutenant Commander Ewen Montagu, a British naval intelligence officer, and Charles Cholmondeley of Britain's MI5 intelligence service, found its "host" in early 1943 when a Welshman living in London committed suicide by taking rat poison. The substance produced a chemical pneumonia that could be mistaken for drowning. The two operatives gave the deceased man a new, documented identity: "Major William Martin" of the Royal Marines.

They literally kept the "major" on ice while arrangements for his new mission were made. To keep Spanish authorities from conducting an autopsy—which would give away the body's protracted post-mortem condition—the agents decided to make "Major Martin" a Roman Catholic, giving him a silver cross and a St. Christopher medallion. They dressed the body, complete with Royal Marine uniform and trench coat, and gave him identity documents and personal letters (including a swimsuit photo of his "fiancée," an intelligence bureau secretary). With a chain used by bank couriers, they fixed the briefcase to his body.

The documents Martin was carrying were carefully prepared to show Allied invasions being planned for Sardinia and Greece (the latter bearing the code name Operation Husky). They also indicated that an Allied deception plan would try to convince Hitler that the invasion would take place in Sicily (the site of the real Operation Husky). With everything in order, the agents carefully placed the corpse into a sealed container—dry ice kept the body "fresh" for the ride out to sea.

The submarine HMS *Seraph* carried "Major Martin" on his final journey. On April 28, the *Seraph* left for the Andalusian coast, and two days later the body of a Royal Marine officer washed ashore. Within days, photographs of the major's documents were on their way to Abwehr intelligence agents in Berlin.

Taking the Bait

Abwehr, Hitler, and the German High Command swallowed the story. After the war, British intelligence determined that Martin's documents had been opened and resealed before being returned by the Spanish. The German General Staff, believing the papers to be genuine, had alerted units in the

Mediterranean to be ready for an invasion of Sardinia and Greece. They moved one panzer division and air and naval assets off the Peloponnese, and disputed Italian fears of an impending invasion of Sicily.

The Allied forces captured Sicily in July and August 1943, and after the war, Commander Montagu wrote a bestselling account of Operation Mincemeat titled, *The Man Who Never Was*. The book was made into a film thriller a few years later.

Who was Major William Martin? The original body appears to have been a 34-year-old depressed Welsh alcoholic named Glyndwr Michael, and "Major Martin's" tombstone in Spain bears Michael's name. Some historians have debated the identity of "Major Martin," however, theorizing that a "fresher" corpse from a sunken aircraft carrier must have been substituted closer to the launch date.

Whoever the real "Major Martin" may have been, one thing is certain: He saved thousands of lives, and became a war hero and action movie star in the process—quite an accomplishment for a dead man!

Female Espionage Agents: Working Undercover for the Allies

In Europe in the 1940s, the "invisibility" of women often made them ideal operatives. They could eavesdrop in public or witness encounters with authorities unnoticed. Britain's Special Operations Executive (SOE) realized that female agents could be especially effective in the field.

Hedgehog

When France fell in 1940, Marie-Madeleine Fourcade helped establish a partisan resistance group called Alliance. Headquartered near Vichy, the group became known as "Noah's Ark" after Fourcade gave its members the names of animals as their code names. Her own code name was "Hedgehog."

The group worked to obtain information about the German armed forces and passed the intelligence on to the SOE. The Alliance was among the first partisan groups organized with the help of the SOE, which supplied the French operatives with shortwave radios and millions of francs dropped by parachute. Although Fourcade was one of the Alliance's top agents, she was caught four times by the Germans; she escaped or was released each time. Once she was smuggled out of the country in a mailbag. On another occasion, she escaped from prison by squeezing through the bars on the window of her prison cell.

While Fourcade's luck held, other members of Noah's Ark were captured in 1944 during a partisan operation aiding the Allied advance in Alsace. They were later executed at the Natzweiler-Struthof concentration camp in France. Fourcade survived the war and wrote a book about her experiences, *Noah's Ark*, published in 1968. She died in a military hospital in Paris in 1989 at age 79.

Louise

Born to a French mother and an English father, Violette Bushell Szabo joined SOE after her husband, a Hungarian serving in the Free French Army, was killed at the Battle of El Alamein. She was given the code name "Louise." Following intensive espionage training, Szabo parachuted into France near Cherbourg on April 5, 1944. On her very first mission, she studied the effectiveness of resistance, and subsequently reorganized a resistance network that had been destroyed by the Nazis. She led the group in sabotage raids and radioed reports to the SOE specifying the locations of local factories important to the German war effort.

Szabo returned to France on June 7 and immediately began coordinating partisans to sabotage communication lines. The Germans captured her three days later, reportedly after she put up fierce resistance with her Sten gun. Szabo was tortured by the SS and then sent to Ravensbrück concentration camp, where she was executed on February 5, 1945 at age 23. Three other female members of the SOE were also executed at Ravensbrück: Denise Bloch, Cecily Lefort, and Lilian Rolfe. Szabo became the second woman to be awarded the George Cross (posthumously) and was awarded the Croix de Guerre in 1947.

Palmach Paratroops

Haviva Reik and Hannah Senesh were Eastern European Jews who joined the SOE to help liberate their homelands from Nazi occupation. Reik was born in Slovakia and grew up in Banska-Bystrica, in the Carpathian Mountains. Senesh, a diarist, poet, and playwright, was born in Budapest. The daughter of a well-known playwright and journalist, she enjoyed a comfortable, secular life before discovering Judaism as a teenager. Both women immigrated to Palestine in 1939 and joined the Palmach, a paramilitary branch of the Zionist Haganah underground organization. Trained as parachutists, Reik and Senesh were 2 of more than 30 Palestinian Jews dropped behind German lines to perform secret SOE missions.

In March 1944, Senesh parachuted into Yugoslavia and, with the aid of local partisans, entered Hungary. She was almost immediately identified by an informer and arrested by the Gestapo. "Her behavior before members of the Gestapo and SS was quite remarkable," a comrade later wrote. "She constantly stood up to them, warning them plainly of the bitter fate they would suffer after their defeat." Though brutally tortured, she refused to give up her radio codes. On November 8, she was executed by a firing squad. "Continue the struggle till the end, until the day of liberty comes, the day of victory for our people," were her final written words.

In September 1944, Reik and four other agents parachuted into Slovakia to aid an uprising against the Fascist puppet government installed by the Nazis, and assist the Jews in the passage to Palestine. Back in her native Banska-Bystrica, she aided refugees, helped Jewish children escape to Palestine, and joined resistance groups in rescuing Allied POWs.

In October, Nazis occupied the town. A few days later, Haviva and her comrades were captured in their mountain hideout by Ukrainian Waffen-SS troops. On November 20, they were executed. The remains of Reik, Senesh, and five other SOE agents were buried in Israel in 1952, in the Israeli National Military Cemetery on Mount Herzl in Jerusalem.

Code Name "Diane"

Her real name was Virginia Hall. She so excelled at her duties that she became a marked woman by the Gestapo and ultimately was awarded the U.S. Distinguished Service Cross. "The woman who limps is one of the most dangerous Allied agents in France," proclaimed German wanted posters, showing a young brunette American. "We must find and destroy her." So dangerous was Virginia Hall's position that even her wooden leg was given a code name, "Cuthbert." Escaping France by crossing the Pyrenees on foot in November 1942, Hall cabled London that "Cuthbert is giving me trouble, but I can cope." Misunderstanding that Cuthbert was another agent, a Special Operations Executive (SOE) officer cabled back, "If Cuthbert is giving you trouble have him eliminated."

Born in Baltimore, educated at Radcliffe and Barnard colleges, and fluent in French and German, Hall had aspired to a Foreign Service career and worked at the U.S. Embassy in Warsaw in 1931. Her hopes were dashed a year later when she accidentally shot herself during a hunting trip in Turkey and her left leg was amputated. In Paris at the outbreak of World War II, Hall volunteered for the French Ambulance Service Unit. When France fell to Germans in June 1940, Hall trekked to London and volunteered for British intelligence.

During 15 months of SOE service, Hall was instrumental in Britain's effort to bring aid to the French resistance. Working from Vichy, she posed as an American journalist while securing safe houses, setting up parachute drop zones, and helping rescue downed Allied airmen. After the United States entered the war, Hall went underground. Her position became untenable when German troops occupied Vichy following Rommel's defeat in North Africa. She barely escaped to Spain.

Back in Britain, Hall volunteered for the U.S. Office of Strategic Services (OSS) and trained in Morse code and wireless radio operation. Unable to parachute because of her leg, she landed in Brittany by British patrol boat prior to the D-Day invasion. Code-named "Diane," she contacted the French Resistance in central France and helped prepare attacks supporting the Normandy landings.

Still hunted by the Gestapo, Hall adopted an elaborate disguise as a French milkmaid, layering her fit physique with heavy woolen skirts that hid her limp. Peddling goat cheese in city markets, she listened in on the conversations of German soldiers to learn the disposition of their units. Hall helped train three battalions of partisan fighters that waged a guerrilla campaign against the Germans and continued sending a valuable stream of intelligence until Allied troops reached her position in September 1944.

After the war, President Truman awarded Hall the Distinguished Service Cross, though she turned down a public presentation to protect her cover for future intelligence assignments. In 1951, she joined the CIA as an intelligence analyst and retired in 1966. She died in Rockville, Maryland, in 1982.

The Catcher Was a Spy

When it comes to character assessments, you gotta listen to Casey Stengel. And the Ol' Perfessor claimed Moe Berg was just about "the strangest man ever to put on a baseball uniform." But Berg wasn't just strange in a baseball uniform, he was strange and mysterious in many ways—some of them deliberate.

Moe Berg lived a life shrouded in mystery and marked by contradictions. He played alongside Babe Ruth, Lefty Grove, Jimmie Foxx, and Ted Williams; he moved in the company of Norman Rockefeller, Albert Einstein, and international diplomats; and yet he was often described as a loner. He was well-liked by teammates but preferred to travel by himself. He never married, and he made few close friends.

"The Brainiest Guy in Baseball"

Moe was an intelligent kid from the beginning, with a special fondness for baseball. As the starting shortstop for Princeton University, where he majored in modern languages, Moe was a star. He was fond of communicating with his second baseman in Latin, leaving opposing base runners scratching their heads.

He broke into the majors in 1923 as a shortstop with the Brooklyn Robins (later the Dodgers). He converted to catcher and spent time with the White Sox, Senators, Indians, and Red Sox throughout his career. A slow runner and a poor fielder, Berg nevertheless eked out a 15-season big-league career. Pitchers loved him behind the plate: They praised his intelligence and loved his strong, accurate arm. And while he once went 117 games without an error, he rarely nudged his batting average much past .250. His weak bat often kept him on the bench.

Berg earned his law degree from Columbia University, attending classes in the off-seasons and even during spring training and partial seasons with the White Sox. When Berg was signed by the Washington Senators in 1932, his life took a sudden change. In Washington, Berg became something of a society darling, delighting the glitterati with his knowledge and wit. Certainly it was during his Washington years that he made the contacts that would serve him in his espionage career.

Time in Tokyo and on TV

Berg first raised eyebrows in the intelligence community at the start of World War II when he shared home movies of Tokyo's shipyards, factories, and military sites, which he had secretly filmed while on a baseball trip in 1934. While barnstorming through Japan along with Ruth, Lou

Gehrig, and Foxx, Berg delighted Japanese audiences with his fluency in their language and familiarity with their culture. He even addressed the Japanese parliament. But one day he skipped the team's scheduled game and went to visit a Tokyo hospital, the highest building in the city. He sneaked up to the roof and took motion picture films of the Tokyo harbor. Some say those photos were used by the U.S. military as they planned their attack on Tokyo eight years later. Berg maintained that he had not been sent to Tokyo on a formal assignment, that he had acted on his own initiative to take the film and offer it to the U.S. government upon his return. Whether or not that was the case, Berg's undercover career had begun.

On February 21, 1939, Berg made the first of several appearances on the radio quiz show *Information, Please!* He was an immense hit, correctly answering nearly every question he was asked. Commissioner Kenesaw Mountain Landis was so proud of how intelligent and well-read the second-string catcher was that he told him, "Berg, in just 30 minutes you did more for baseball than I've done the entire time I've been commissioner." But Berg's baseball time was winding down; 1939 was his last season.

Secret Agent Man

Berg's intellect and elusive lifestyle were ideal for a post-baseball career as a spy. He was recruited by the Office of Strategic Services (predecessor to the CIA) in 1943 and served in several capacities. He toured 20 countries in Latin America early in WWII, allegedly on a propaganda mission to bolster the morale of soldiers there. But what he was really doing was trying to determine how much the Latin countries could help the U.S. war effort.

His most important mission for the OSS was to gather information on Germany's progress in developing an atomic bomb. He worked undercover in Italy and Switzerland and reported information to the States throughout 1944. One of his more daring assignments was a visit to Zurich, Switzerland, in December 1944, where he attended a lecture by German nuclear physicist Werner Heisenberg. If Heisenberg indicated the Germans were close to developing nukes, Berg had been directed to assassinate the scientist. Luckily for Heisenberg, Berg determined that German nuclear capability was not yet within the danger range.

Life After the War

On October 10, 1945, Berg was awarded the Medal of Freedom (now the Presidential Medal of Freedom) but turned it down without explanation. (After his death, his sister accepted it on his behalf.)

At the end of the war he was recruited by the CIA. It is said that his is the only baseball card you will find inside CIA headquarters. After his CIA career ended, Berg never worked again. He was often approached to write his memoirs. When he agreed, in 1960 or so, the publisher hired a writer to provide assistance. Berg quit the project in fury when the writer indicated he thought Berg was Moe Howard, founder of the Three Stooges. But his unusual career turns were later immortalized in the Nicholas Dawidoff book *The Catcher Was a Spy*. At age 70, Berg fell, injuring himself. He died in the hospital. His last words were to ask a nurse, "What did the Mets do today?"

Benjamin Franklin: Secret Agent?

Benjamin Franklin was a man of many roles: inventor, scientist, publisher, philosopher, diplomat, and one of America's founding fathers. But could he also have been a spy?

French Connection

Franklin was rumored to be involved in French espionage activities during the American Revolution. While most say that Benjamin Franklin was spying for the Americans, some claim that Franklin was in league with the British.

In September 1776, Congress appointed Franklin, Silas Deane, and Thomas Jefferson commissioners to France to plead the American cause in its war against Great Britain. Jefferson declined, but Franklin (despite the fact that he was 70 years old) and Deane agreed.

One of the most celebrated people on the planet, Franklin could hardly slip into France unnoticed. Almost from the moment he arrived, he was surrounded by a web of intrigue. Spies surrounded Franklin at every turn. French police chief Jean-Charles Lenoir ran an organized and efficient spying operation in Paris, which was so riddled with spies that it was said when two Parisians talked, a third inevitably listened. In addition to being tailed by the French, the British ambassador to France was also following Franklin's every move.

The Spy Who Stayed Cold

Every week, like clockwork, secret messages were sent from Franklin's residence to British intelligence, keeping them abreast of everything Franklin was planning, doing, or talking about. While Franklin was certainly involved in this undercover war, was he aware of these notes? Was he the source of them? Or was this all part of Franklin's own master plan? Franklin could hardly have been unaware of the situation. Soon after he arrived in France, a Philadelphian living in Paris had warned Franklin to be wary. In a letter she wrote, "You are surrounded with spies who watch your every movement."

His reply has become legendary. "I have long observed one rule . . . to be concerned in no affairs I should blush to have made public, and to do nothing but what spies may see and welcome." He did nothing to tighten security, which led John Adams to believe that Franklin was, at best, senile, and at worst, criminally careless. Franklin even claimed that he would not dismiss his valet, Edward Bancroft, even if he were "a spy, as probably he is."

Double-Aught-Seven
If Franklin wasn't a British spy, was he spying for America? Biographer James Srodes believes this to be a more plausible scenario, and notes that mid-20th century CIA director Allen Dulles concluded that Franklin had set up a spy network inside the British government. However, his assumption lacks documentation. As Srodes notes, Franklin hardly needed a ring of secret informants in London; he had many friends inside the British government, any of whom could feed him valuable information.

"The important thing about intelligence is not how it is obtained but how it is used," says Srodes. Franklin used information obtained from England to force the French to move quickly to the aid of American rebel forces. He then turned around and casually let it be known how much France was aiding America, which disturbed the British.

This much we know: Franklin had indeed been close to someone who was a spy. Decades later it was revealed that his valet was indeed spying for America—and for England. We may never know whether or not Bancroft's boss, Ben Franklin, was also a spy, or even for what side. However, what we do know is that Benjamin Franklin was certainly a cagey American.

Spies for Dixie

Though it lacked many of the resources that the North had, the South had a healthy stable of spies during the Civil War.

The Socialite Spy

Although she was already in her mid-40s by the time the Civil War erupted, Rose O'Neal Greenhow—a seductive Washington socialite and widow—used her wiles to keep Confederates informed of Northern movements.

Before the Civil War, Mrs. Greenhow had been known to entertain international diplomats and members of Congress, and she had been close to President James Buchanan. But when the Southern states started to secede, her regional sympathies prevailed, and soon she was enlisted to collect covert intelligence for the new Southern government. Befriending Colonel E. D. Keyes— who just happened to be the secretary to Union General-in-Chief Winfield Scott—Greenhow gained information that led directly to the Southern victory in the first major action of the war, the First Battle of Bull Run, in July 1861. For her efforts, officials in Richmond sent her a personal note of thanks.

In January 1862, Greenhow was arrested as a spy and, after a few months of house arrest, sent to Old Capitol Prison in Washington, D.C. Even from jail, however, she continued to collect Union secrets and pass them to the Confederates, hiding messages in a ball of yarn or a visitor's hair bun to transport the precious information.

Released in exchange for Union prisoners, Greenhow was exiled to the Confederacy and arrived in Richmond in June to a hero's welcome. Confederate President Davis personally received her party upon its arrival. But now that she was known in the North, her career as a spy in America was over. Davis sent Greenhow to Europe, where she sought political and financial support for the Confederacy.

In September 1864, Greenhow was returning to America aboard the blockade runner *Condor*. During a fierce storm, the *Condor* was pursued by a Northern ship and ran aground. Greenhow tried to escape by rowboat but was thrown overboard. Weighed down by more than $2,000 in gold, Greenhow drowned. Her body later washed ashore, and she was buried with full military honors in Wilmington, North Carolina.

The Covert Chaplain

Thomas N. Conrad was one of the Confederacy's most ambitious and effective spies. His initial plans included assassinating Union General-in-Chief Winfield Scott and kidnapping President Lincoln.

Prior to the war, Conrad had been headmaster at Georgetown College in Washington, D.C., but his enthusiasm for the South proved to be too much: He was arrested in June 1861 when he had "Dixie" played as the graduation's processional march. Upon his release, he signed up as a chaplain with General Jeb Stuart's Confederate troops in Virginia. As a man of the cloth, Conrad easily made his way into Union territory, where he was able to garner Union strategies and plans.

As the war wound down, Conrad returned to Washington, where he changed his hairstyle and shaved his beard. It was a look that made him a dead-ringer for John Wilkes Booth; in fact, Conrad was mistaken for Booth and briefly arrested for Lincoln's assassination.

Conrad returned to the academic world after the war, teaching at Rockville Academy in Maryland and at Virginia A & M, becoming president there in 1881. He recorded his adventures in his memoir, *The Rebel Scout*, and died in 1905.

A Confederate Charmer

As a courier for Rose O'Neal Greenhow, Antonia Ford held many parties for Union officers and soldiers at her home in Fairfax Court House, Virginia. Ever the socialite, she would charm her guests, who didn't realize she was collecting military information for the Confederates.

She became a favorite resource for General Stuart and was named an honorary aide-de-camp. She also provided Colonel John Mosby and his rangers with critical and timely information that led to the kidnapping of Union General Edwin H. Stoughton in March 1863. Her luck couldn't last, however, and Ford accidentally blew her cover to a member of a northern detective agency. She was arrested only days later.

A charmer to the end, Ford became involved with her Union jailor in the Old Capitol Prison, Major Joseph Willard. The Major proposed, they married, and she signed a Union loyalty oath in 1864. Prison life had made its mark on Ford, however, leaving her sickly and weak. She died in 1871 at age 33.

The Squirrel Hill Spy

Laura Ratcliffe was also a valuable aide to Colonel John Mosby and his rangers, who often used her home in Squirrel Hill, Pennsylvania, for clandestine meetings. Ratcliffe allowed Mosby to use a large rock there as a rendezvous where Confederates could exchange messages and keep money taken from Union plunder.

Ratcliffe was active in Confederate espionage throughout the war but was never caught. Later in life, she married a Union veteran named Milton Hanna. When she passed away in 1923, Ratcliffe's wake was set up in the front window of her house. Hundreds of people showed up to pay their last respects.

Allan Pinkerton—Spying for the Union Cause

The exploits of Allan Pinkerton during the Civil War paved the way for the Secret Service. In a letter to President Lincoln dated April 21, 1861, detective Pinkerton offered his services and commented on one of the traits that would make him an icon of law enforcement for generations. "Secrecy is the great lever I propose to operate with," he wrote.

Establishing the Eye

Born in Scotland in 1819, Allan Pinkerton came to the United States in 1842. He originally was a barrel builder by trade, but his skills at observation and deduction led him to a career fighting crime. By age 30, he'd joined the sheriff's office of Cook County, Illinois, and been appointed Chicago's first detective. He later joined attorney Edward Rucker to establish the North-Western Police Agency, a forerunner of the Pinkerton Agency. As his corporate logo, Pinkerton chose an open eye, perhaps to demonstrate that his agents never slept. Clients began calling him "The Eye."

Pinkerton and his operatives were hired to solve the growing number of train robberies, which became more and more of a problem as railroads expanded across the nation. George B. McClellan, president of the Ohio and Mississippi Railroad, took particular notice.

Wartime Duties

In 1861, Pinkerton's agency was hired to protect the Philadelphia, Wilmington, and Baltimore Railroad. In the course of their responsibilities, Pinkerton and his agents learned of a pre-inaugural plot to kill President-elect Lincoln. The detectives secretly took Lincoln into Washington before he was scheduled to arrive, thwarting the conspirators. Lincoln was inaugurated without incident.

When the war began, Pinkerton was given the duty of protecting the president. He was also put in charge of gathering intelligence for the army, now run by his old railroad boss, McClellan. The detective and his operatives infiltrated enemy lines. Using surveillance and undercover work, both new concepts at the time, agents gathered vital information. Pinkerton tried to get details any way he could. His people interviewed escaped slaves and tried to convince literate slaves to return to the South to spy. He used female spies, and he even infiltrated the Confederacy himself several times using the alias Major E. J. Allen.

Uncertain Information

While much of this was invaluable, his work was tarnished by a seeming inability to identify enemy troop strengths. His reports of enemy troops were detailed, including notes on morale, supplies, movements, and even descriptions of the buttons on uniforms. Yet the numbers of troops he provided were highly suspect.

In October 1861, as McClellan was preparing to fight, Pinkerton reported that Confederate General Joseph Johnston's troops in Virginia were "not less than 150,000 strong." In reality, there were fewer than 50,000. The next year he reported the strength of Confederate General John Magruder at Yorktown, putting troop numbers at about 120,000 when the true number was closer to 17,000.

After the true strength of these forces was discovered, Pinkerton was ridiculed. Some historians believe that Pinkerton was unaware of the faulty information, but others insist he intentionally provided inflated figures to support McClellan's conservative battle plans. The truth will likely never be known, as all of Pinkerton's records of the war were lost in the Great Chicago Fire of 1871.

Return to Civilian Life

After McClellan, one of Pinkerton's staunchest supporters, was relieved of his command by Lincoln, Pinkerton curtailed his spying activities and shifted his work back toward criminal cases, which included the pursuit of war profiteers. He ultimately returned to Chicago and his agency, working until his death in 1884.

Agent 488: Carl Jung and the OSS

World War II called individuals from all walks of life to duty—even famous scientists had parts to play. In America, Einstein wrote Roosevelt to suggest the possibility of an atomic bomb. In Germany, Wernher von Braun raced to build rockets for his country. And in Switzerland, Carl Jung used his own talents to offer the world a glimpse into the psyche of a madman.

Services in Demand

In the 1930s, Germany had a reputation as a hotbed of scientific innovation across a variety of disciplines. The Nazis were quick to take advantage of much of this research in the form of technologically advanced weapons, but they did view one particular field with suspicion: psychology. The most well-known figure in this science was Sigmund Freud, who was Jewish—and although they were interested in the topic itself, the Nazis couldn't very well make use of a Jewish scientist.

One alternative was Carl Jung. He was Swiss, of German extraction, and well respected in the field. Moreover, he had written about the psychological differences inherent in groups of people, and anything that supported tribal or racial divisions was of interest to the Nazis. They went so far as to suggest that Jung relocate, and even discussed arresting him on a visit to Berlin just to keep him in Germany. He firmly declined the invitation, as he also did with an offer to migrate to the United States, preferring to remain in touch with his roots. Unfortunately, the German invitation gave rise to a rumor that he was a Nazi sympathizer, an accusation he called "an infamous lie."

His accusers needn't have worried. He "despised politics wholeheartedly" and had little use for Hitler or any other leader except, perhaps, as an interesting study in the psychology of power. His independence may have contributed to a request he received in October 1939 from Nazi doctors, who asked if he would be willing to examine the Führer; Hitler had been behaving erratically, and his personal doctors were worried. Jung turned down the invitation, already convinced that the German leader was at least half crazy. He went on to offer the opinion that both Hitler and the German people were possessed, but his invectives were directed at both sides—he once referred to Roosevelt as the "limping messenger of the apocalypse" and believed that the president had all the makings of a dictator.

Recruiting Agent 488

Regardless of the views he harbored about both leaders, Jung did contribute to the Allied cause. In 1942, American agent Allen Dulles (who would go on to head the CIA) arrived in Berne, Switzerland, which he used as a base to monitor German activities. Dulles enlisted the aid of an American expatriate of some local notoriety, Mary Bancroft, who eventually also became Dulles's lover. Bancroft had been a patient of Jung's, and the two had formed a mutual attachment. Knowing of their association, Dulles began posing questions to the famous psychologist through Bancroft, soliciting his opinion on "a weekly, if not daily basis."

The two eventually met, and Dulles continued to rely on Jung to analyze various events. Jung's responses found their way into Dulles's reports to the OSS, with Jung listed as the source under the code name "Agent 488." Of particular interest was Jung's insight into the personality of the Nazi leaders, especially of Hitler. Dulles urged the OSS to pay particular attention to Jung's analysis of the Führer, which included the opinion that Hitler was capable of anything up until the very end, at which point Jung could not "exclude the possibility of suicide in a desperate moment."

Jung's analysis, of course, proved correct: Hitler became increasingly unstable as the war progressed, eventually taking his own life, trapped in his own bunker. After the conflict, the records detailing Jung's full involvement were strictly classified, but Allen Dulles offered one evaluation: "Nobody will probably ever know how much Professor Jung contributed to the Allied cause during the war."

Code Breakers Crack the Enigma

Enigma was the code name for a portable cipher machine used by Germany to encrypt and decrypt secret messages. Invented in 1918 by a German engineer named Arthur Scherbius, the machine was initially marketed to businesses as a way of preventing corporate espionage. By 1933, the German Army, Navy, and Air Force were producing their own modified versions of the machine. With hundreds of millions of letter combinations, the German military thought the code was unbreakable.

How Did It Work?

Enigma encoded messages by performing sequential substitutions using electrical connections. The machine resembled a typewriter; it had 26 keys—one for each letter of the alphabet.

When a key was depressed, an electrical impulse traveled through a plug board at the front of the machine to a rotor contact inside the machine. The surface of each rotor also contained 26 electrical contacts, again representing letters of the alphabet. Each contact was wired to a key on the keyboard as well as to a contact on the next rotor. An output device illuminated the cipher letter the system created. The rotors were interchangeable, and extra rotors could be added. Enigma also used a device called a reflector, which redirected the electrical impulses back through the machine a second time. The code was exceedingly complex.

The Enigma was small enough to be carried into the field, but it required three men to operate: One typed the coded message into the machine, a second recorded the encrypted output one letter at a time, and a third transmitted the result in Morse Code.

Poland's Big Break

In 1932, Poland's intelligence corps received a package from its French counterparts containing Enigma guidelines that had been obtained by a German intelligence clerk named Hans-Thilo Schmidt. Schmidt was later arrested by the Nazis for the theft; he probably committed suicide in 1943 while in prison for treason.

Using some of Schmidt's information and a commercial version of the Enigma, three of Poland's brightest cryptanalysts successfully recreated the Enigma code and its indicator system in 1933. Though the commercial version was much different from the machines used by the German Army and Navy, Marian Rejewski, Henryk Zygalski, and Jerzy Rozycki deduced the internal wiring of Enigma's rotors. They used advanced mathematics, exploiting the German error of repeating the message setting (a three-letter sequence at the beginning of the transmission). The Poles developed two electromechanical machines that functioned similarly to the machines the Germans were using to decipher messages.

The Germans increased the sophistication of Enigma in 1939. By July of that year, Poland felt its independence threatened. The Polish Cipher Bureau gave its French and British counterparts all of its research in the hopes their teams could crack the new German code. The British had great success.

Britain's Best and Brightest

In 1939 the British intelligence community organized its code-breaking operations north of London at an estate called Bletchley Park. The British department operating out of the English manor was referred to as the Government Code and Cipher School. Staff at Bletchley Park consisted of chess experts, mathematicians, linguists, computer scientists, and even crossword enthusiasts. They made several important discoveries, allowing them to break the Enigma code even when it was altered every two days. Their success was due in part to German methods of coding:

🦆 The reflector ensured that no letter could be coded as itself.

🦆 Because the keyboard contained only letters, all numbers had to be spelled out.

🦆 Military ranks, military terms, and weather reports appeared often, making it easier to decode these words.

🦆 The Germans would not repeat rotor order within a month, and the rotors changed position every two days. This greatly reduced the combinations used in the machines by the end of the month, making it easier to crack those messages.

The Allies eventually captured several German U-boats and surface ships with intact Enigmas and codebooks, giving the code breakers the knowledge they needed to correctly anticipate changes to the code. By 1943, most coded German communications were read routinely.

To Act, or Not to Act

Intelligence gleaned from the decrypted Enigma messages fell under Ultra, the code name used by Britain, and later the United States. The codes of the Luftwaffe were the first broken by Britain's team of cryptologists, and Britain monitored the Luftwaffe traffic to learn of planned raids during the Battle of Britain. Cryptologists also alerted Prime Minister Churchill to the fact that Germany wanted air superiority before launching an invasion of Britain. Messages intercepted between Rommel and Hitler revealed some of Rommel's planned tactics in Africa, giving the Allies an edge at Alam Halfa.

Cracking the Enigma was perhaps most useful to convoys crossing the Atlantic. As codes were broken and manuals captured, the Allies were able to locate and avoid U-boat patrols. While the breaking of the Enigma code did not win the war for the Allies, there can be no denying the feat shortened the war, saving many lives in the process.

Film Noir

Hardboiled gumshoes and treacherous dames, pervasive corruption and irresistible temptation, deceit, betrayal, and murder—these are the trappings of film noir, a dark and nihilistic genre of film that evolved in Hollywood in the 1940s and has remained influential ever since.

Film noir arose from two unrelated storytelling forms. In the period between the two world wars, American pulp novels by writers such as Raymond Chandler, Dashiell Hammett, and James M. Cain explored a shadowy world of second-rate private detectives and marginalized drifters who were drawn into a web of crime. During that same time, the German film industry was fascinated with a dark style of moviemaking known as Expressionism that featured distorted sets and stark contrasts between light and shadow. Many German filmmakers immigrated to America in the late 1920s and early 1930s, and they and their new Hollywood colleagues applied the Expressionist visual style to those hardboiled American crime dramas. The result was a perfect match of theme and visual style that would come to be known as film noir.

The Conventions

At the dark heart of every film noir lies a mystery and a protagonist seeking to untangle it. Invariably, the mystery proves to be deeper and more disturbing than it first appeared, and the filmmaker's true purpose in sending the hero on this journey is to reveal the widespread corruption and moral decay that characterizes modern society.

To that end, the hero is typically a flawed figure who lacks the capacity to untangle the web of deceit he is surrounded by. Instead, he is a pawn to the whims of the conspirators who run the show and doesn't come to fully understand their machinations until it's too late. And his greatest threat comes not from gun-toting thugs or the corrupt powerbrokers who control them but from the beautiful and provocative woman who seduces and betrays him—the femme fatale.

Visually, noir films are characterized by the highly controlled use of lighting. Settings are frequently dominated by shadows that create a barred motif or weblike pattern, suggesting that the characters are hopelessly trapped.

Rain-slicked streets crowded with neon signs become menacing pathways of alternating dark and light, and skewed camera angles suggest a world gone awry. These distorting visual techniques convey the world as an endless maze from which there is no chance of escape.

Film noir also often employs nonlinear narrative, meaning that events in the story are revealed to the viewer out of chronological order, which contributes to the disorienting feel of the films. The classic *Out of the Past* (1947) starring Robert Mitchum and Jane Greer—often named as one of the best examples of the genre—makes heavy use of this technique to convey the idea that the characters can never escape their past. *The Killers* (1946), Burt Lancaster's debut film, offers one of the most extreme examples of this. The film opens with the death of the main character and then proceeds to tell the sorry tale that led to his violent end.

The Classics

Though the classic period of the genre lasted less than 20 years (from the early 1940s to the late 1950s), there are plenty of excellent examples for movie buffs to choose from, such as *Double Indemnity* (1944) with Fred MacMurray and Barbara Stanwyck; *Scarlet Street* (1945) starring Edward G. Robinson and Joan Bennett; *The Big Sleep* (1946) with Humphrey Bogart and Lauren Bacall; and *Kiss Me Deadly* (1955) starring Ralph Meeker.

Primed to Be a Private Eye

Think being a PI is all high-speed chases and sultry suspects? Actually, for the most part, working as a private investigator can be a lot like any job—you stare blankly at a computer screen in a dimly lit cubicle for eight hours a day—only for less money. But the good news is that working in the private investigation field can be just about anything you make of it—just look at Thomas Magnum!

Questionable Origins

The first private eye on record was a French criminal and privateer named Eugene Francois Vidocq, who founded a private investigation firm in 1833. But Vidocq was hardly a man with a spotless record, and neither were his employees: Most of his investigators were his friends who were ex-convicts and other citizens of questionable character. Vidocq was periodically arrested by the police on a series of trumped-up charges, but he was always released after they failed to produce enough evidence to support their claims. Despite his questionable background, Vidocq made a number of significant contributions to the field of investigation, including record keeping, ballistics, indelible ink, and unalterable bond paper.

The Modern PI

Fast forward to recent statistics from the U.S. Department of Labor, which state that in 2014, there were approximately 35,000 working gumshoes. While more than a third of working private investigators have college degrees, many have only high school diplomas or Associate degrees, and some have neither. Those with college degrees come from varied backgrounds, such as accounting, computer science, business administration, or the dozens of other majors whose curriculum lends itself to specific types of investigative work. Interestingly, most private investigators do not have a degree in criminal justice.

The Nature of the Work

Talk to anyone who's knowledgeable about the private investigation business and they'll tell you that the prerequisites for success are an unquenchable thirst for answers and the ability to root out details after everyone else has given up. Superior communication skills and a special area of expertise, say, in computers, also come in handy. The most successful private eyes are people who can think logically, apply their unique knowledge to a problem, and consistently come up with creative means to their ends.

A Day in the Life

Depending on their background, private investigators can end up working for a variety of employers: individuals, professional investigative firms, law firms, department stores, or bail bondsmen. Many set up their own private practice. One place they can count on *never* working is for the local police department or the FBI. Government agencies rarely interface with private investigation firms. Unfortunately, that nixes the dramatic movie image of a lone-wolf PI getting a call in the middle of the night because the police are stumped and desperately need help.

The type of work private investigators do is largely dependent on the type of company they work for, the types of cases they take, and what their clients ask of them. The majority of cases have to do with locating lost or stolen property, proving that a spouse has been unfaithful, finding missing friends or relatives, conducting background investigations, or proving that a business associate absconded with the company cash.

Much of the work that private investigators do involves long hours sitting behind the wheel of their car doing surveillance with binoculars and cameras with telephoto lenses. Only the highest- profile cases involving investigative firms with large operating budgets can afford sophisticated surveillance vans loaded with high-tech equipment. Other cases require collecting facts the old- fashioned way: by interviewing suspects, witnesses, and neighbors in person. Facts that can't be collected that way are often obtained by perusing public records by computer, or researching tax records, business licenses, DMV records, real estate transactions, court records, and voter registrations.

The PI Paycheck

But how much can a private eye expect to make? Fortunately (or unfortunately, whatever the case may be), the entertainment industry has painted a rather broad picture of the private investigation business. For every television show about a PI living on a Hawaiian estate, there's another show about a PI living in a dilapidated trailer house on the beach. Back in 2015, the median salary for private investigators was around $48,000 and it hasn't changed much since. Top earners in the field handle the industries of finance, insurance, and government, while investigators focusing on retail typically earn the lowest wages.

Still Want to Be a Private Eye?

For those who remain undaunted by the proposition of drinking their dinner out of a thermos and spending ten hours a day in a car or cubicle for sometimes as little as fast food wages, here's some insight on how to pursue a career in private investigation.

Many private investigators have retired early from military, police, or fire department careers. Having pensions or retirement funds can help with "getting over the hump" until the earnings as a PI increase.

Some states require specific schooling while others require new investigators to spend time completing on-the-job training before applying for their license. Most states have licensing requirements for becoming a PI, so it's important to look into what's required and how long it takes before one can expect to begin to make a decent living. If the type of work requires that private investigators carry a firearm, a private eye will need to look into the local ordinances for carrying a concealed weapon.

If nothing else, private investigation can certainly be a fascinating and challenging career that promises a break from the ordinary job doldrums. So grab that Beretta, rev up that Ferrari, and get ready for your new life as a gumshoe!

The Real "Spy vs. Spy"

People love a good story involving intrigue and conflict. One enduring tale has run for over 40 years in the form of a much-beloved comic strip called "Spy vs. Spy."

Hidden Meanings

"Spy vs. Spy" was the brainchild of Cuban political cartoonist Antonio Prohias. The artist came up with the idea for the wordless strip during the late 1950s as a means of expressing his political views and to call attention to the rapidly escalating Cold War.

In the strip, two spies—who look identical, except one is all dressed all in black and the other all in white—portray two opposing (though never stated) agendas and constantly attempt to sabotage each other through a series of creative schemes and inventions. Prohias never really informed his readers whom the characters represented, leaving fans free to figure it out for themselves. Occasionally the strip will introduce a third, grey-clad female spy (thus becoming "Spy vs. Spy vs. Spy"), who inevitably becomes the central point of the conflict as the two suitors battle for her affection.

The Man Behind the MAD Comic

Prohias began drawing the "Spy vs. Spy" comic shortly after he fled his native Cuba for the United States in 1960. After Cuban dictator Fidel Castro took over the last "free press," Prohias feared that his days were numbered. He spent his days working in a garment sweatshop and drew the strip in his kitchen at night. The wacked-out *MAD* magazine picked up the continuing series; soon Prohias was able to devote all of his time to drawing comics and honing his technique. Still, he was always aware of the comic's origins. In a clever nod to his underground days, he would sign "By Prohias" in Morse code underneath the title: -* * * -* --* --* * -* ---* * * * * * * -* * * .

After creating over 500 comics, Prohias relinquished the project to the *MAD* magazine staffers in 1990. He died on February 24, 1998. But his work lives on: Although the Cold War has ended, fans of the strip still continue to enjoy the antics of Prohias's two hapless spies.

CHAPTER 11

Watch Out for the Whopper

The Hitler Diaries Hoax

Adolf Hitler was an ambitious politician, but when it came to writing, he could be pretty darn lazy. After the success of *Mein Kampf*, the first volume of which was published in 1925 and the second in 1926, he seemed content to rest on his laurels, even if those laurels were in a cozy cell in Landsberg prison. Surely such a significant figure would leave behind a greater written legacy than that. This literary lethargy would eventually make historians very cranky—and very gullible.

The Roots of the Hoax

Though Hitler did halfheartedly pen a 200-page sequel to *Mein Kampf* in 1928, he grew bored with the project and never bothered to have it published. In fact, only two copies existed, and those were kept under lock and key by Hitler's order. This manuscript was discovered by American troops in 1945, but though authenticated by several of Hitler's associates, the writings were considered to be mostly inflammatory Nazi propaganda and simple rehashings of *Mein Kampf*. For these reasons, the book was never published widely.

Hitler was literally a "dictator," relying on secretaries to take down his ideas and plans. Often, even Hitler's most grandiose and terrible commands—such as the one to destroy European Jewry—were given only verbally. Historians were also frustrated by the dearth of personal correspondence that could be linked to Hitler. His mistress, Eva Braun, was not the brightest woman to ever walk the face of the earth, and their letters have not been found.

Fertile Ground for a Fake

This lack of primary-source material is what made the Hitler diaries hoax such a success at first. A staff reporter at West Germany's *Stern* magazine, Gerd Heidemann, fell for the ruse hook, line, and sinker, and saw the publication of the diaries as a way of advancing his stalled career in journalism. He convinced his editors at *Stern* that the journals were real, and they paid 9.3 million marks (about 6 million U.S. dollars at that time) for the first serial rights. On April 25, 1983, *Stern* hit the streets with a sensational cover story: "Hitler's Diary Discovered." Media outlets around the world were more than happy to follow *Stern*'s lead, and the *New York Times*, *Newsweek*, and the *London Sunday Times* all immediately jumped on the huge story.

The editors at *Stern* certainly should have been more wary of Heidemann's story, as he was known to be obsessed with Hitler and the Third Reich. He had a passion for acquiring Nazi collectibles of almost any sort, even emptying his bank account to buy Hermann Göring's dilapidated private yacht. However, Heidemann's enthusiasm was so contagious, and the demand for all things Hitler so great, that it seems his superiors simply couldn't resist. But from whom had Gerd Heidemann obtained the diaries? And where had they been all these decades?

Fabricating the Führer

Konrad Kujau had started forging documents as a youth in East Germany, but he really hit his stride after defecting to West Germany and setting up an antiquities store in

Stuttgart. Kujau was brazen and seemingly fearless in his work. He made and sold "genuine" Nazi items that sound ludicrous now and should have raised alarms for his clients then: Who could believe, for example, that Hitler had once written an opera? Yet his customers wanted to believe, and as long as Kujau shunned publicity, he was able to make a nice living off their ignorance and inexperience. After all, these were private collectors who wanted to hold onto their purchases as investments. But Kujau got greedy, and maybe just a little hungry for fame. Enter *Stern* reporter Heidemann, sniffing for a story.

In 1981, Kujau showed Heidemann 62 volumes of what he claimed were Hitler's diaries, dated from 1932 to 1945. Heidemann was astonished and asked Kujau about their history; how had such important documents remained hidden and unknown for so many years? Kujau was ready with a plausible-sounding (to Heidemann, at least) explanation: Nazi flunkies had tried to fly Hitler's personal belongings, including the diaries, out of Berlin, but the plane had been shot down and crashed in Dresden, its cargo surviving without any major damage. Conveniently for Kujau, Dresden was now behind the Iron Curtain, so his claim of obtaining the volumes one at a time from an East German general could not easily be confirmed or disproved. But if anyone longed to believe, it was Heidemann.

Media Circus

The publication of the diaries was an international bombshell, with historians, journalists, politicians, and antiquities dealers lining up to take sides in the media. Some historians immediately pointed out Hitler's aversion to writing in longhand, but others, such as the esteemed British World War II expert Hugh Trevor-Roper, declared the diaries to be authentic. On the day the story was published, *Stern* held a press conference in which Trevor-Roper, along with German historians Eberhard Jackel and Gerhard Weinberg, vouched for the documents. It would be a mistake all three would grievously regret.

The media uproar only intensified when, less than two weeks later, it was revealed beyond any question that the Hitler diaries were forged. Not only were the paper and ink modern, but the volumes were full of events and times that did not jibe with Hitler's known activities and whereabouts. Kujau was so careless in his fakery that he didn't even bother to get the monogram on the title page right: It read FH rather than AH. Some observers pointed out that the German letters F and A are quite similar, but surely as a German himself, Kujau would have known the difference. The best conjecture is that the diaries were sloppily prepared for his usual type of client—a dullish foreigner who wouldn't ask too many questions—and that Heidemann's arrival on the scene turned what might have been just another smooth and profitable transaction into a worldwide scandal.

Off to the Clink

Heidemann was arrested and tried for fraud, and Kujau was arrested and tried for forgery. Both men wound up serving more than four years in prison. However, Kujau reveled in his celebrity after his release, appearing on talk shows and even selling paintings as "genuine Kujau fakes." But although Kujau tried to treat his forgeries as a lighthearted joke, it should be noted that had he not been unmasked, the diaries could have done real damage. Perhaps most serious—the document claimed that Hitler had no knowledge of the Holocaust.

The Death of Davy Crockett

You can start fights in Texas suggesting that the Alamo fighters—Davy Crockett was prominent among them—didn't die fighting to the last man. But do we really know that they did?

First, the orthodox version: Davy Crockett grew up rough and ready in Tennessee, wrestling bears, tramping the wilderness, and otherwise demonstrating his machismo. He went into politics, lost an election, and moved to Texas. His homespun, informal braggadocio went over just fine in what would soon become the self-proclaimed Republic of Texas. Mexico, of course, didn't grant that Texas had the right to secede. General Antonio López de Santa Anna invaded the Republic and cornered a group of its defenders in Alamo Mission, San Antonio de Béxar (now just San Antonio). Shortly before independence, Crockett had signed on to fight for Texas.

Why question that? Most of the questions stem from the memoir of a Mexican officer who fought there, Jóse Enrique de la Peña. De la Peña says that seven captives, including Crockett, were brought before Santa Anna and murdered in cold blood after the battle. He also says that Crockett took refuge in the Alamo as a neutral foreigner rather than as a volunteer militiaman. That poses authenticity problems, because there was no logical reason for Crockett to be at the Alamo unless he planned to fight in its defense.

It's worth noting that de la Peña says he found the execution appalling. However, the Mexican officer also tells an implausible version of the death of Colonel William Travis, commander in charge of the siege of the Alamo: He claims to have seen it occur, but there's little chance de la Peña could have positively identified Travis at a distance. This was, after all, a battle with thick black-powder smoke, hand-to-hand combat, and concealment.

What evidence supports the orthodox version? Travis's slave, Joe, survived the battle and says Travis died defending the north wall (not where de la Peña has him). Joe also says he saw Crockett's body surrounded by dead Mexican soldiers, and an officer's wife who survived also testifies that Crockett died in battle. Santa Anna himself didn't say anything about executing Crockett in his after-action report; he did say that Crockett's body was found along with those of other leaders, and he didn't make a big deal of that.

Why is it contentious? The memory of the Alamo is a Texan cultural rallying point: That's why it's folklore. Opposing this view is a revisionist stance that seems so ready to dismiss tales of military valor that it dumps the orthodox account as too simple and perfect to be true. Either side has generally drawn a conclusion and seeks evidence to support it.

What do we know? So much happened at Alamo Mission between February 23 and March 6, 1836, that we will never know. It is plausible that some wounded survivors, possibly dying, were executed after the battle; that doesn't negate anyone's heroism. What's lacking is compelling, credible evidence to contradict the eyewitnesses who report no such thing. Absent that evidence, and with de la Peña's writing a questionable account well after the fact, the weight of documentation suggests that Davy Crockett went down fighting.

A Fictional Tale and Its Nonfictional Response

Elan Gale is a TV producer from Los Angeles, California, who apparently decided to produce his own little story when he was on a US Airways flight during Thanksgiving in 2013.

Gale tweeted several times about a woman named Diane, who was supposedly sitting in seat 7A and was being rude to flight attendants. Eventually, he retaliated by writing her a nasty note on a napkin. He took a photo of it, and also posted it to Twitter.

The "fight" continued, with Gale tweeting things like, "I'm not going to lie, I am shaking. This is so terrifying. She is so angry at me it's kind of incredible," and describing his fellow passenger as "in her late forties or early fifties. She is wearing mom jeans and a studded belt and she is wearing a medical mask over her idiot face."

Diane eventually wrote her own note, and Gale tweeted more barbs and insults. All the while, Gale's Twitter followers grew from thirty thousand to around one hundred thousand, with people cheering him on and praising him for his tactics. The alleged fight culminated after the flight ended, with Gale tweeting, "Well, Diane just slapped me."

Four days later, Gale took to Twitter again to reveal that the entire sequence of tweets had been a hoax. There was no passenger named Diane. He simply made everything up for its entertainment value. But the really disturbing thing about Gale's Thanksgiving tweets is just how many people jumped on his bandwagon and cheered him on. Gale was publicly berating a stranger—whether imaginary or not—who his followers knew nothing about. His Twitter audience heard only his side of the story, yet they applauded his rude insults and jumped to the conclusion that Diane deserved everything she got.

The Grumpy Old Man

Urban myths, stereotypes, and stock characters—they never seem to go away. Maybe because they sometimes hold a grain of truth?

Take the Grumpy Old Man. You may never have met one, but you know he says things like "get off my lawn," and "that's not how we did it in my day." You know he doesn't like you. He doesn't like anything, really. And he likes it that way. And whether you like it or not, researchers confirm that grumpy old men are no stereotype.

The English Longitudinal Study of Ageing surveyed nearly ten thousand people ages fifty-five and older and asked them to rate themselves in areas such as health, finances, and overall happiness. Across the board, men reported lower levels in quality of life than did women. Why? Are old men uncomfortable in those pants? Does the hair growing from their ears and nostrils irritate them?

"Remember when I asked for your opinion about going shirtless? Me neither."

The answer may be male menopause. Also known by its clinical name, andropause (or the snicker-inducing hypogonadism), male menopause is caused by testosterone deficiency. Some men experienced diminished testosterone production in their forties; full decline occurs in the early fifties. The symptoms include flaccidity in a certain body part and an unwillingness to get it on. (See some connection here?) Irritability, depression, and loss of sleep are other signs. Treatments range from simple life changes—such as increased exercise, improved diet, and lowering stress—to chemical enhancements that include elevating testosterone levels through injections or supplements.

Johnny Appleseed: Too Good to Be True?

The legend is almost too glib. What kind of person would run around planting apple trees? Didn't he need a job? It turns out that trees were Johnny Appleseed's business—but a gentler businessperson never lived. His real name was John Chapman, and he is one of those rare folk heroes whose legend is fact. What's more, he deserves all the reverence his memory enjoys.

🦆 Johnny was born in 1774, and his first memories were of the Revolution. His father was a farmer, a Revolutionary officer, and veteran of Bunker Hill; Johnny was just seven years old when Lord Cornwallis hung it up at Yorktown.

🦆 His mother died young. Relatives raised Johnny and his sister. Perhaps with his father away at war and in the care of family members, he grew up not really thinking of any place as a permanent home—he may have been primed to be a natural roamer.

🦆 Johnny went west in 1792. By the end of the 1790s, he was a nurseryman: He picked the seeds out of apples, planted them, grew saplings, and sold them to new settlers.

Because many Continental veterans received land grants in the Ohio Valley, lots of people in Pennsylvania and Ohio wanted fruit trees.

🦆 Johnny may have been the closest thing to a Jainist monk in U.S. frontier history. He tried hard to avoid killing any insect, much less any animal.

🦆 He didn't just wander around tossing seeds at random. Johnny Appleseed was a savvy businessperson, though he usually wore cast-off clothing and went barefoot. He would get the seeds for free from cider mills, plant a nursery, fence it, and then leave it in a neighbor's charge. Johnny would show up every so often to check on the orchards. If the neighbor had collected any payment for saplings, Johnny would pick that up.

🦆 Chapman was a Swedenborgian. That's a religious affiliation. There are still members of the church around today (and they sure revere Chapman). Emmanuel Swedenborg was an 18th-century Swedish genius and Christian mystic whose church could best be described as non-mainstream Protestantism with an occult streak.

🦆 Johnny never married and apparently had no children. When anyone asked him why he wasn't married, he told them he believed he would have two great wives in Heaven, provided he didn't marry on Earth.

🦆 Why didn't someone else plant more trees and push him out of business? Johnny had a knack for showing up just before major population waves. Ask any skilled businessperson: It is partly about marketing, partly about finance, and all about timing and location. By the time most people arrived, Johnny's trees were ready for sale and transplant. Some are still standing today.

🦆 As much money as Chapman brought in through his business skill, he left most of it on the table. If people couldn't pay him cash, he took goods in barter or sold on credit. He tended to forgive bad debt. During his life, he tried very hard to give his wealth away.

🦆 Along with apples, Johnny planted many and varied medicinal herbs wherever he went. Fennel, a licorice-smelling perennial often used as a spice, was referred to as "Johnny Weed" back in those days.

🦆 In areas where relations with Native Americans could at times be tense, Johnny Appleseed walked in complete safety. Not only did the tribes respect him, some thought him touched by the Great Spirit. He seemed to be a man without an enemy.

🦆 If you lived in the Ohio Valley and liked a drink now and then, you'd have had good reason to toast John's health. Most of his apples were made into cider. And Johnny definitely enjoyed a drink and a pinch of snuff, relaxing for an evening with a traveling or settled family, or any stranger who happened to be around.

🦆 An early animal rescuer, Johnny would buy neglected horses and find them good homes or put them out to graze and see if they got well. If they did, he would foster them, extracting a promise of good treatment.

🦆 Chapman was also a Swedenborgian missionary. He donated a considerable portion of his assets to the church, spent a lot of his money on Swedenborgian literature, and tried his best to spread his faith as he traveled.

🦆 As if that weren't enough, John Chapman was a deeply patriotic man whose oratory would have served him well in politics, had he cared for such things. He loved Fourth of July festivals and always found time to participate.

🦆 Johnny "Appleseed" Chapman passed away on March 18, 1845, near Fort Wayne, Indiana. And for once the folktale is less impressive than the reality.

The Men on the Moon

On July 20, 1969, millions of people worldwide watched in awe as U.S. astronauts became the first humans to step on the moon. However, a considerable number of conspiracy theorists contend that the men were just actors performing on a soundstage.

The National Aeronautics and Space Administration (NASA) has been dealing with this myth for nearly 40 years. In fact, it has a page on its official Web site that scientifically explains the pieces of "proof" that supposedly expose the fraud. These are the most common questions raised.

If the astronauts really did take photographs on the moon, why aren't the stars visible in them? The stars are there but are too faint to be seen in the photos. The reason for this has to do with the fact that the lunar surface is so brightly lit by the sun. The astronauts had to adjust their camera settings to accommodate the brightness, which then rendered the stars in the background difficult to see.

Why was there no blast crater under the lunar module? The astronauts had slowed their descent, bringing the rocket on the lander from a maximum of 10,000 pounds of thrust to just 3,000 pounds. In addition, the lack of atmosphere on the moon spread the exhaust wide, lowering the pressure and diminishing the scope of a blast crater.

If there is no air on the moon, why does the flag planted by the astronauts appear to be waving? The flag appears to wave because the astronauts were rotating the pole on which it was mounted as they tried to get it to stand upright.

When the lunar module took off from the moon back into orbit, why was there no visible flame from the rocket? The composition of the fuel used for the takeoff from the surface of the moon was different in that it produced no flame.

Conspiracy theorists present dozens of "examples" that supposedly prove that the moon landing never happened, and all of them are easily explained. But that hasn't kept naysayers from perpetuating the myth.

Twenty-three years after the moon landing, on February 15, 2001, Fox TV stirred the pot yet again with a program titled *Conspiracy Theory: Did We Land on the Moon?* The show trotted out the usual array of conspiracy theorists, who in turn dusted off the usual spurious "proof." And once again, NASA found itself having to answer to a skeptical but persistent few.

Many people theorize that the landing was faked because the United States didn't have the technology to safely send a crew to the moon. Instead, it pretended it did as a way to win the final leg of the space race against the Soviet Union. But consider the situation: Thousands of men and women worked for almost a decade (and three astronauts died) to make the success of *Apollo 11* a reality. With so many people involved, a hoax of that magnitude would be virtually impossible to contain, especially after almost four decades.

For additional proof that the moon landing really did happen, consider the hundreds of pounds of moon rocks brought back by the six missions that were able to retrieve them. Moon rocks are unique and can't just be fabricated, so if they didn't come from the moon, what is their source? Finally, there's no denying the fact that the astronauts left behind a two-foot reflecting panel equipped with dozens of tiny mirrors. Scientists are able to bounce laser pulses off the mirrors to pinpoint the moon's distance from Earth.

The myth of the faked moon landing will probably never go away. But the proof of its reality is irrefutable. In the words of astronaut Charles Duke, who walked on the moon in 1972 as part of the *Apollo 16* mission: "We've been to the moon nine times. Why would we fake it nine times, if we faked it?"

The First Flag Raising on Iwo Jima

Each year, more than 30,000 people compete in the Marine Corps Marathon, which finishes next to Arlington Cemetery, the resting place of American war dead just outside Washington, D.C. As runners climb the final hill near the finish line, they're inspired by the Marines Corps War Memorial, the 60-foot-high statue of leathernecks raising a flag over Iwo Jima's Mount Suribachi. Few realize the iconic image depicts not the first but the second flag that was hoisted at Iwo Jima.

The famous emblem raising took place shortly after noon on February 23, 1945. The first raising happened about 90 minutes earlier.

For four days, thousands of U.S. Marines had been killed or wounded while storming the beaches and battling toward the volcanic mount that dominated the island. Recalled 24-year-old Corporal Charles W. Lindberg, one of the first flag's raisers, "The Japs had the whole beach zeroed in. Most of the fire was coming from Suribachi."

Capturing Mount Suribachi

Lieutenant Colonel Chandler W. Johnson commanded the 2nd Battalion, 28th Regiment, 5th Marine Division. His task was to capture the top of Suribachi. On the morning of February 23, after one of Johnson's companies scouted a path to the crest, he assigned the mission to 40 marines from 2nd Battalion's Company F. Johnson and gave the company commander, First Lieutenant Harold G. Schrier, an American flag, measuring 54 by 28 inches. "If you get to the top," Johnson told Schrier, "raise it."

One of the patrol's members was Sergeant Ernest Ivy Thomas. On February 21, two days before the flag was raised, Thomas had taken command of his rifle platoon when its leader was wounded. Armed with only a knife when his rifle was shot away, he repeatedly braved enemy mortars and machine guns while directing tanks against pillboxes at the base of Suribachi. Thomas was awarded the Navy Cross for his actions.

Led by Lieutenant Schrier, the patrol began its climb at 0800 hours on February 23, with Lindberg lugging his 72-pound flamethrower. They reached the top at 1015 and were attacked by a small Japanese force. While the skirmish continued, Thomas and another man scrounged up a 20-foot-long iron pipe. At 1020, recalled Lindberg, "We tied the flag to it, carried it to the highest spot we could find, and raised it." Hoisting the ensign was Lindberg, Thomas, and Schrier, along with Sergeant Henry O. "Hank" Hansen, Private First Class Louis C. Charlo, and Private First Class James Michels.

The First Photo

Sergeant Lou Lowery, a photographer for *Leatherneck* magazine, took a photo of It. While he snapped the picture, a Japanese soldier tossed a grenade nearby. Just in time, Lowery threw himself over the crater's lip. He landed 50 feet below, his camera lens smashed, yet his film remained intact. After the raising, "All hell broke loose below," remembered Lindberg. "Troops cheered, ships blew horns and whistles, and some men openly wept."

"Make It a Bigger One!"

On the beach was Secretary of the Navy James Forrestal, who'd arrived to watch the capture of Suribachi with Marine Commander General Holland "Howlin' Mad" Smith. Forrestal told Smith: "Holland, the raising of that flag on Suribachi means a Marine Corps for the next five hundred years." According to the book *Flags of Our Fathers* by James Bradley, Forrestal requested the emblem as a souvenir.

Battalion chief Johnson was not pleased. "The hell with that!" he reacted. He ordered an operations officer, Lieutenant Ted Tuttle, to have another patrol secure the flag and replace it with another banner. "And make it a bigger one," he told Tuttle.

Soon after, as Lowery climbed down from Suribachi, he ran into three fellow photographers going up: Marines Bob Campbell and Bill Genaust, and the Associated Press's Joe Rosenthal, whose photo of the second flag raising garnered him the Pulitzer Prize. The three photographers were considering going back down the mount, but Lowery told them the summit offered good views, so they kept trudging up. At the top, Schrier had the first flag lowered at the same time the second 96-by-56-inch flag was raised. Down on the sands, most never noticed the switch.

The Battle Raged On

The terrible battle continued. Of the 40 marines in the first patrol, 36 were later killed or wounded on Iwo Jima. Private First Class Charlo, grandson of a noted Flathead Indian chief, was killed March 2, and Sergeant Thomas died on March 3. Photographer Genaust had taken a video of the second flag raising with imagery similar to Rosenthal's; his film was featured in a famous newsreel. He was killed March 4. Altogether, close to 7,000 marines died and 19,000 were wounded.

On March 1, Lindberg was wounded on Suribachi and was awarded the Silver Star. "I was after a mortar position up there, and I was shot, and it shattered my arm all to pieces," Lindberg said. Back in the States, he was angered by his patrol's lack of recognition. "I went on home and started talking about this," he stated. "I was called a liar and everything else. It was terrible." But "it was the truth," he said. "I mean, everyone says, 'Iwo Jima flag raising,' they look at the other one."

The Japanese were also bitter, with good reason—they had lost the battle. Iwo Jima was part of the prefecture of the city of Tokyo. Its loss meant that the U.S. Marines had secured their first piece of official Japanese soil. The rest of Japan beckoned.

Nessie Nix

In 1934, London surgeon Robert Kenneth Wilson sold a photograph he had taken while on a birding expedition to the *London Daily Mail*. In the photo, the long slender neck of an unknown animal rises from the water of Scotland's Loch Ness.

Wilson's story held for 60 years until 1994, when a Loch Ness Monster believer named Alastair Boyd uncovered evidence that the photograph was a hoax. It turned out that in 1933, the *Daily Mail* had hired big-game hunter Marmaduke Wetherell to investigate reported sightings at Loch Ness and find the monster. Instead of Nessie, however, Wetherell found tracks that had been faked with a dried hippo foot. Working with his son and stepson, Wetherell staged the Loch Ness photograph in revenge, attaching a head and neck crafted from plasticine to the conning tower of a toy submarine. A friend convinced Wilson to be the front man.

It was Wetherell's stepson who broke the story, admitting his part in the hoax to Boyd in 1994. However, Wetherell's son Ian had published his own version of the hoax in an obscure article in 1975.

Outrageous Media Hoaxes

Man on the Moon

In 1835, in one of America's earliest media hoaxes, *The New York Sun* reported that a scientist had seen strange creatures on the moon through a telescope. The story described batlike people who inhabited Earth's neighbor.

...ers couldn't get enough of the story, so other publish- ers scrambled to create their own version. When faced with criticism, *The Sun* defended itself, stating that the story couldn't be proven untrue, but eventually the stories were revealed as hoaxes.

Hoaxer Ben Franklin

For nearly a decade, Ben Franklin perpetrated a hoax con- tinually claiming that Titan Leeds, the publisher of the main competitor to Franklin's *Poor Richard's Almanac*, was dead. This greatly decreased Leeds's circulation, since no one wanted to read the ramblings of a dead man. Leeds pro- tested, but year after year, Franklin published annual memorials to his "deceased" competitor. When Leeds really did pass away, Franklin praised the man's associates for finally admitting he was dead.

Anarchy in London

In 1926, a dozen years before *The War of the Worlds*, the BBC staged a radio play about an anarchic uprising. The "news- cast" told of riots in the streets that led to the destruction of Big Ben and government buildings.

The population took the play so seriously that the military was ready to put down the imaginary rioters. The following day the network apologized and the government assured the public that the BBC would not be allowed such free range in the future. The British were ridiculed worldwide, especially in the United States, where the public had not yet been introduced to a young actor named Orson Welles.

Mr. Hearst's War

Media mogul William Randolph Hearst had no problem with manipulating the truth to sell newspapers. One of his most famous hoaxes was a series of misrepresentations of what was really occurring in Cuba during the lead-up to the Spanish–American War. He sent artist Frederic Remington to the island to capture the atrocities, but the artist found none. "You furnish the pictures, I'll furnish the war," Hearst replied. But Hearst's misuse of pictures was not limited to that event. Consumed with a passion to defeat the communists, he once ordered his editors to run pictures showing an imaginary Russian famine. However, on the same day, they unwittingly published truthful stories about the rich harvest Russia was enjoying.

Poe's Prank

Though Edgar Allan Poe is best known for his macabre works of fiction, he had his hand in a few works of journalistic fiction as well. One of his best known was a piece that ran in *The New York Sun* in 1844, the same year he wrote his classic poem "The Raven." The article claimed that daring adventurer Monck Mason had crossed the Atlantic Ocean in a hot air balloon. Mason had only intended to cross the English Channel but had been blown off course and arrived 75 hours later in South Carolina. When readers investigated the claim, Poe and *The Sun* conveniently admitted they had not received confirmation of the story.

Millard Fillmore's Bathtub Bunk

Everyone seems to know that Millard Fillmore was the first president to have a bathtub installed in the White House. The only problem is, it isn't true. The story, along with a detailed history of the bathtub, was all a hoax perpetrated by writer H. L. Mencken when he worked for *The New York g Mail.* "The success of this idle hoax, done in time of war, when more serious writing was impossible, vastly astonished me," Mencken later wrote. The excitement around his piece and the public's inability to accept the truth affected Mencken, and he began to wonder how much of the rest of history was indeed, in his words, "bunk."

The Master Forger

"Monet, Monet, Monet. Sometimes I get truly fed up doing Monet. Bloody haystacks." John Myatt's humorous lament sounds curiously Monty Pythonesque, until you realize that he can do Monet—and Chagall, Klee, Le Corbusier, Ben Nicholson, and almost any other painter you can name, great or obscure. Myatt, an artist of some ability, was probably the world's greatest art forger. He took part in an eight-year forgery scam in the 1980s and '90s that shook the foundations of the art world.

Despite what one might expect, art forgery is not a victimless crime. Many of Myatt's paintings—bought in good faith as the work of renowned masters—went for extremely high sums. One "Giacometti" sold at auction in New York for $300,000, and as many as 120 of his counterfeits are still out there, confusing and distressing the art world. But Myatt never set out to break the law.

Initially, Myatt would paint an unknown work in the style of one of the cubist, surrealist, or impressionist masters, and he seriously duplicated both style and subject. For a time, he gave them to friends or sold them as acknowledged fakes. Then he ran afoul of John Drewe.

The Scheme Begins

Drewe was a London-based collector who had bought a dozen of Myatt's fakes over two years. Personable and charming, he ingratiated himself with Myatt by posing as a rich aristocrat. But one day he called and told Myatt that a cubist work the artist had done in the style of Albert Gleizes had just sold at Christies for £25,000 ($40,000)—as a genuine Gleizes. Drewe offered half of that money to Myatt.

The struggling artist was poor and taking care of his two children. The lure of the money was irresistible. So the scheme developed that he would paint a "newly discovered" work by a famous painter and pass it to Drewe, who would sell it and then pay Myatt his cut—usually about 10 percent. It would take Myatt two or three months to turn out a fake, and he was only making about £13,000 a year (roughly $21,000)—hardly worthy of a master criminal.

One of the amazing things about this scam was Myatt's materials. Most art forgers take great pains to duplicate the exact pigments used by the original artists, but Myatt mixed cheap emulsion house paint with a lubricating gel to get the colors he needed. One benefit is that his mix dried faster than oil paints.

The Inside Man

But Drewe was just as much of a master forger, himself. The consummate con man, he inveigled his way into the art world through donations, talking his way into the archives of the Tate Gallery and learning every trick of provenance, the authentication of artwork. He faked letters from experts and, on one occasion, even inserted a phony catalog into the archives with pictures of Myatt's latest fakes as genuine.

the years went by, Myatt became increasingly wor-
ed about getting caught and going to prison, so at last he
told Drewe he wanted out. Drewe refused to let him leave,
and Myatt realized that his partner wasn't just in it for the
money. He loved conning people.

The Jig Is Up

The scam was not to last, of course. Drewe's ex-wife went
to the police with incriminating documents, and when the
trail led to Myatt's cottage in Staffordshire, he confessed.

Myatt served four months of a yearlong sentence, and
when he came out of prison, Detective Superintendent
Jonathan Searle of the Metropolitan Police was waiting for
him. Searle suggested that since Myatt was now infamous,
many people would love to own a real John Myatt fake. As
a result, Myatt and his second wife Rosemary set up a tidy
business out of their cottage. His paintings regularly sell for
as much as £45,000 ($72,000).

Charming Charlatans

The only thing mystifying about snake charmers is their
cunning ability to bamboozle. Here's what's really happen-
ing when a cobra "dances" to the music.

Strolling past a bazaar in India, you spot a man sitting cross-
legged in front of a basket. After he raises a flute and begins to play, a venomous cobra starts to sway, rhythmically
"dancing" to the music. You look on, mesmerized. At times
the serpent is mere inches from the snake charmer's face;
indeed, the man even fearlessly "kisses" it. The man and his
music seem to have a calming effect on the surly serpent.

In truth, it doesn't require much nerve to charm a cobra, and here are the dynamics behind the demonstration. Contrary to folklore, the much-feared cobra is not aggressive. In fact, it will try to scare off potential predators rather than fight them. A cobra accomplishes this by standing erect and flaring its hood. When it sets its sights on a potential threat, it will sway its body along with the motions of the intruder. Sound familiar?

A snake charmer knows this behavior well—and capitalizes on it. To get a cobra to rise from a basket and stand erect, the performer simply lifts the lid. Startled by the sudden light, the serpent emerges. But before the cobra will "dance" along with the flute music, it must first be conditioned to regard the instrument as an enemy (the performer will often tap the snake with it during "training" sessions). Once accomplished, the snake will follow the flute's every move.

The Story of the Tasaday

In 1972, a *National Geographic* article announced the discovery of a gentle, pristine Stone Age people in the Philippines: the Tasaday. Skeptics say the Tasaday were a hoax perpetrated by the Marcos government—but are they right?

The Discovery

In 1971, strongman Ferdinand Marcos was dictator of the Philippines. His wealthy crony, Manuel Elizalde, Jr., was head of Panamin, a minority-rights watchdog agency. In a nation with 7,107 islands, 12 major regional languages, and hundreds of ethnic groups, such an agency has its work cut out for it. The Philippines' second largest island, Mindanao,

is bigger than Maine, with lots of jungle. According to Elizalde, a western Mindanao tribesman put him in contact with the Tasaday. The tribe numbered only a couple dozen and lived amid primitive conditions. Their language bore some relation to nearby tongues but lacked words for war and violence. They seemed to be living in gentle simplicity, marveling at Elizalde as a deity and protector. For his part, Elizalde clamped the full power of the Philippine state into place to shield his newfound people. One of the few study groups permitted to examine the Tasaday was from *National Geographic*, which introduced the Tasaday to the world in 1972.

After Marcos fell from power in 1986, investigators studying the lives of the Tasaday revealed that it was all a fraud. According to reports, Elizalde had recruited the Tasaday from long-established local tribes and forced them to role-play a Stone Age lifestyle. The Tasaday eventually became the "Tasaday Hoax."

A Scam Revealed?

A couple of Tasaday told a sad story: They normally farmed nearby, living in huts rather than caves, but Elizalde made them wear loincloths and do dog-and-pony shows for paying visitors. The poorer and more primitive they looked, the more money they would get. In one instance, a group of German journalists who set out to document the Tasaday found them dressed primitively—sort of. They were wearing leaves, but they had stuck them onto their clothing, which was visible beneath the foliage. Scientific skeptic... soon surfaced as well: How could they have remained that isolated for so long, even on Mindanao? Why didn't modern disease now decimate them? Why did their tools show evidence of steel-knife manufacturing?

Elizalde didn't back down easily. In an attempt to keep up the charade, he flew a few Tasaday to Manila to sue the naysayers for libel. With Marcos ousted, however, Elizalde was less able to influence investigators or control what they had access to. Eminent linguist Lawrence Reid decided that the Tasaday were indeed an offshoot of a regional tribe—but one that had been living in the area for only 150 years, not more than a thousand as was claimed. Likely as confused as everyone else at this point, previous Tasaday whistleblowers now confessed that translators had bribed them to say the whole thing was a hoax.

The Aftermath

Elizalde later fled to Costa Rica, squandered his money, and died a drug addict. If he had indeed fabricated the history of the Tasaday, what was his motivation? It could have been a public-relations ploy, because the Marcos government had a well-earned reputation for repression. A strong minority-rights stance in defense of the Tasaday could be expected to buff some tarnish off the government's image. Commerce likely played a role, for the Tasaday episode denied huge tracts of jungle to logging interests. Perhaps those interests hadn't played ball with Marcos and/or Elizalde.

Elizalde did not "discover" the Tasaday, but that doesn't mean they were total fakes. What Is clear Is that they were pawns in a sociopolitical chess game far greater than the jungle of Mindanao.

Come to Beautiful Greenland!

Greenland, perhaps best known as the largest island that is not a continent, sits way up in the north Atlantic near the Arctic Circle. Ninety percent of the island is covered by an ice cap and smaller glaciers—which means that the place is mostly uninhabitable. Although the northern coasts of Greenland have been settled for thousands of years by the Inuit (the same folks who brought you the igloo), the island was largely unknown to Europeans until the late tenth century.

How did a country that boasts almost no green land get the name Greenland? Theories abound, including the legend that Iceland switched names with Greenland to avoid being invaded by barbarians. But many historians believe that Greenland's name may be a part of one of the biggest—and earliest—marketing scams of all time. In the tenth century, a Viking named Erik the Red fled his home of Iceland after committing murder. Erik took the opportunity to explore the islands and lands to the west of Iceland.

Drifting across the Atlantic, Erik eventually came to the rocky coast of an enormous island that was covered in ice. He had an idea: If he couldn't be with his people, then he'd bring his people to him. Though only a sliver of land was actually green, he promptly named the island Greenland, which, according to the Icelandic sagas, was because "men will desire much the more to go there if the land has a good name." Some Icelanders, believing the marketing hype, came and settled along the southern coast of Greenland, where they flourished for several hundred years. To be fair to Erik, archaeologists believe that the island's climate was a bit more temperate during the Vikings' heyday than it is now. Still, calling this arctic landmass Greenland is a bit like a modern-day housing developer grandly naming its cookie-cutter development Honey Creek, even though the only "creek" nearby is a sewage canal. At any rate, Erik the Red pulled off one heck of a real-estate swindle.

It Came with a Monster of a Hangover Too

In an unintentional hoax that mimicked America's famed "War of the Worlds" radio broadcast, an entire city in northern China was emotionally traumatized on September 19, 1994, when television warnings were repeatedly broadcast to viewers in Taiyuan. In a scrolled message, viewers were warned about the gruesome Sibuxiang Beast, a creature with a deadly bite. "It is said that the Sibuxiang is penetrating our area from Yanmenguan Pass and within days will enter thousands of homes," read the ominous type. "Everyone close your windows and doors and be on alert!"

With this "official" announcement acting as impetus, the good people of Taiyuan launched into a panic as some barricaded themselves inside their homes. Local officials were soon swamped with telephone calls.

It seems it had all been one giant misunderstanding. The Sibuxiang Beast was real enough, but it wasn't an animal. In fact, it was nothing more than a new brand of liquor. The townspeople had, in fact, been watching a commercial.

The ad's creator was fined about $600 for causing a public panic, but the incident had turned Sibuxiang liquor into a household name virtually overnight. Three months after the incident, the owner reported that his client base had quadrupled.